The Pastor's Pen

ENCOURAGEMENT TO MAKE
YOU A BETTER CHRISTIAN

Dr. Larry L. Charles II

Copyright © 2025, Dr. Larry L. Charles II
Contact the Author: Pastorcharlesthebreath@gmail.com

All rights reserved. No part of this book may be reproduced, stored in a retrieved system, or transmitted in any form or any means, electronic, mechanical, photocopying, recording, scanning, or otherwise, without the prior written permission of the author.

Author: Dr. Larry L. Charles II
Publisher: Kingdom News Publication Services, LLC.
Transcription Services: Denise Bridges

DISCLAIMER
All the material contained in this book is provided for educational and informational purposes only. No responsibility can be taken for any results or outcomes resulting from the use of this material.

While every attempt has been made to provide information that is both accurate and effective, the author does not assume any responsibility for the accuracy or use/misuse of this information.

Printed in the United States of America.
ISBN 978-1-955127-42-4

Preface

Where are you in your walk with Christ? Are you a seasoned saint filled with Godly wisdom, a well-rounded Christian making extraordinary strides in your walk with Christ, or maybe even a new believer filled with passion, excitement, and questions? Wherever this Christian journey may find you today or 20 years from now, this book is filled with Bible-centered, practical teaching that will bless you.

We encourage you to keep your Bible nearby as you read through this book, so you can easily reference the scriptures Dr. Charles mentions while sharing valuable life lessons.

Foreword

Over the past two decades, I've had the privilege of watching Dr. Larry Charles grow from a faithful congregant into a trusted son in ministry. His journey has been marked by humility, perseverance, and a deep love for God's Word and God's people.

The Pastor's Pen is a reflection of that journey—a tapestry woven from years of study, service, and spiritual insight. Dr. Charles writes with the heart of a shepherd and the mind of a scholar, offering wisdom shaped by experience and anchored in grace.

I commend this work to you with joy. May it inspire, challenge, and draw you closer to the One who called him—and calls each of us—to serve.

In Christ's service,
Bishop Charles E. Williams

Inspirational Sentiments

"The Lord has done great things for us, and we are filled with joy." — Psalm 126:3

After more than thirty years of marriage, six children, and eight grandchildren, I can truly say—God has been faithful. Our journey has been one of grace, growth, and unwavering love. I've watched Larry serve with humility, lead with wisdom, and love with strength.

The Pastor's Pen reflects not only his calling, but the life we've built together—a legacy of faith, family, and purpose. I thank God for our union and the story we continue to write.
– **Lady Cheryl E. Charles**

I thank God for Pastor Charles! He continues to affirm and cultivate the high calling of Jesus Christ on my life and the gifts that God has given me. – **Evangelist Erica Whitfield**

Pastor Larry Charles love for the word of God and God's people is evident in his teaching and pursuit to helping others live Godly lives. It's an honor to be under the teaching of Pastor Charles; each encounter with his teaching and preaching has required me to respond to the word of God as taught in James 1:22. – **Minister Rhonda K. Fontonette**

The Word is brought alive through the teachings of Pastor Charles. It may even prick you to want to do better when you know you aren't doing your best. You will be prompted to do better according to the word of God, for me, I rearranged my morning routine to start my day off with the Word. I am thankful for his teachings. – **Minister Erica McGraw**

I have always enjoyed the way that you stay in the Word during your messages. You are always well prepared, and I will always strive to do the same. –**Elder Keith Lewis**

Pastor Larry Charles is someone who is likened unto the Good Shepherd with the rod and staff; a protector, supporter, competent and trustworthy. He comforts the young and old with love and devotion. We are willingly following his lead.
–**Elder Charles & Denise Bridges**

I have known Pastor Charles for over twenty years and can truthfully say that he leads by example. It's a pleasure and honor to serve under his leadership.
–**Deacon James Perkins**

Table of Contents

Chapter 1: How to Have a Good Argument 1

Chapter 2: Don't Eat That 17

Chapter 3: A Change is Coming 35

Chapter 4: Foot Work 51

Chapter 5: How to Defeat Discouragement 67

Chapter 6: The Wrong Way on the Right Road 81

Chapter 7: God's Example of a Good Father 97

Chapter 8: God's Witness Protection Program 109

Chapter 9: Know the Code 124

Chapter 10: Lifting Your Head in Low Places 140

Chapter 11: He's the God of Another Chance 153

Chapter 12: Are You a Self-Serving Sinner 164

Chapter 13: Litte Things Make a Big Difference 179

Chapter 14: The Truth About Trouble 194

Chapter 15: Don't Reject the Invitation 210

Chapter 1
How to Have a Good Argument

Galatians 2:11-21

For the sake of emphasis, but when Peter was come to Antioch, I withstood him to the face because he was to be blamed. This chapter will discuss the components of how to have a good argument, a good old-fashioned argument.

As we all know, disagreements are a part of life. There's an illustration in the Peanuts cartoon where Lucy says to Snoopy, *"There are times when you really bug me, but I must admit, there are also times when I feel like giving you a big hug."* Snoopy looked at her and replied, *"That's me, huggable and buggable."* And just like we hear Snoopy declaring it, so are we. We are all huggable and buggable; there are times when we can get on one another's nerves.

We often think that simply because we become Christians and because we name the name of Christ, and we embrace the principles of Almighty God that surely, we will be exempt from any kind of disappointments or disagreements. But that is not the truth. It doesn't matter how big your Bible is, doesn't matter how many tongues you talk in, nor does it matter how many scriptures you can quote, every now and again, we're all going to disagree. But we have to learn how to be agreeable in our disagreeing. I cannot come to you and be in disagreement with you and begin to accuse you and insult you if I really want to have a good argument. So, I've taken the liberty by the Holy Spirit to introduce to us some ways to effectively deal with conflict.

If truth be told, many relationships don't make it simply because we have not the tools to be able to deal with conflict resolution. We don't know how to get over the issue. So, I curse you, you curse me, and we go our separate ways. Every now and again, something rises up in you and if you're not careful, you'll say some things that you used to say that you thought you would never say again. So, we have to implore God give me the tools to be able to overcome disagreements. So, wherever people are, there will be disagreements.

Recent research shows that hostility only breeds more hostility. Venting negative emotions may clear the air temporarily, but it does not solve the underlying issue. Many times, it serves only to make matters worse. The message becomes clear that since we have been brought in this together, we must learn to fight together so that we will stay together.

Church is not a place where we are exempt from disagreements, but if we are going to be the sheep of the Most-High God, sometimes we might butt one another, but I'm not going to cut you, because I love you and that we can get over this if we learn how to get along.

How to Have a Good Argument

So, let me just share something with you. There are three dimensions to disagreements or conflict. These dimensions are perception, feeling, and action.

The first dimension, perception, is when one person believes that their interests, values or needs are being denied and that another person's value, needs or interests are being given. So, you automatically feel I am being denied and make up in your mind that I will not be denied. I'm going to have what I believe belongs to me. We may say, *"I am in this country, and we believe I've got rights."* And sometimes we bring that into our relationships. So, instead of learning these tools that we need to deal with conflict, we take on the mindset you step on me, I'm going to step on you, but it's your perception.

The second dimension on this journey is your feelings. Anger rests in the bosom of fools according to Ecclesiastes 7:9. Some of us allow anger to just rest on us, to rest in our chest like a boil, and instead of us dealing with anger, the anger deals with us. And we lash out at people that we say we love. We curse and we fuss, and fight because we don't know how to deal with the anger that is resting on us. The Bible says in Ephesians 4:26, *"Let not the sun set on your wrath."* In other words, you've got to release it, or it will deny you some things that God has purposed for your life.

If it's not anger, then it's fear, and we know how fear can deal with us. Fear comes to rule us. We know fear is an acronym for *False Evidence Appearing Real*. And when you operate in fear, you're going to move into a place where you have conflict based on fear. I'm fearful that he's going to use me. I'm fearful that she's going to take advantage of me. I'm fearful that they are denying me my rights on my job. So, instead of you trusting and having faith, fear takes over. We need to know that trust dispels fear. The Bible even says that love, perfect love, casts out all fear. So, I've got to get to the place where I say, *"Lord, if I'm operating in fear, then I'm not operating in love. So, God help me."*

Sadness is another feeling that can trap us. Sadness causes you to be melancholy and downtrodden. It affects your countenance by being cast down; shoulders slumped and feelings of defeat. The reason is that it keeps us from operating where God wants us to operate. He says you can't communicate when your body language is all wrong. If someone comes at you with the wrong body language, you are going to say, *"Oh, well, let me get squared up too."*

The third dimension is your actions. Conflicts ride in on the horse called action. From our body language to our speech to violence. Today, you get into battles on the various social media platforms. You're just battling and they are laughing and you're hotter than a wet hen, and you'll never see these folks. Instead of you just unplugging that stuff and getting away from it, you're there, and you stew over that all day long, and it's ruling you instead of you ruling it. Or not just on social media, but in your house. You get into it with somebody and each of you walk around for three days and don't say anything to each other. You're slamming cabinets and slamming doors. You decide, *"Well, I am not going to say anything to her, and I am not saying anything to him."* They will come in and say good evening, and your response is a mumbled, hmm.

Let's learn from the Apostles what we can do to deal with our circumstances and our situations. In Galatians 2:1, the timespan has been 14 years where we have managed to create two competing opinions about Christianity. We have one opinion of those who are called the way, according to Isaiah 40:3, when it said, *"Prepare ye the way, make a straight path for he who is to come."* When they talk about that, they say, we are of the way because Jesus said in John 14:6, *"I am the way, the truth, and the light."* So, they put the

How to Have a Good Argument

title on themselves. These are the Jews who decided that they were going to follow Christ. They had been circumcised, and they were following the laws, but they believed that Jesus is the Messiah. So, they are of the way. Then we have those who in Acts 11:26, it says that they were first called Christians at Antioch. The Gentiles were in Antioch and didn't have to be circumcised and they could eat some pork. So, they had a bacon sandwich if they wanted, they had some rib tips, and they were enjoying life, saying, *"We are saved even though we eat a little swine."* So, they were going on with a pork chop sandwich with some mustard on it. They were going on about their business and then all of a sudden, they got to Jerusalem and Antioch on opposing ends of the same circumstance.

One is saying, *"You've got to be circumcised and follow the laws."* The other is saying, *"We are not going to be circumcised, and you can keep your laws. Because you are not justified by the works of the law, but you are justified by faith in Jesus Christ."*

So, they said, you're not going to frustrate the grace of God that has been extended to us. We're going to walk in it and if you don't like it, you don't have to come to Antioch. Sometimes we are on opposing ends. Some of you are in Jerusalem, and some of you are in Antioch. You are standing your ground and saying, *"I don't care if anybody likes it, but you don't have to come to Antioch and I don't have to come to your Jerusalem. You stay over there, and I'll stay here. You do you, boo and I'm going to stay over here."*

In the text, we have two different competing leaderships. In Jerusalem, you have Peter, James, and John. While in Antioch, you have Paul, Barnabas, and Titus. So, with these competing viewpoints, it is inevitable that we're going to have some issues. Much like in the body of Christ, people strain at a gnat and swallow a camel. You let these women come to church with earrings on? What is that on their mouth? They got lipstick on. Are you kidding me? She got on a skirt that come all the way to the floor. So, that doesn't have anything to do with it. God doesn't want your garment. He wants your heart, because if He gets your heart, He'll get your garment.

Conflict Resolution

If we want to have conflict resolution, according to the Galatians 2:11-21, what should we do?

First, consider that you don't know it all. This will be the first step to conflict resolution with those in your family and your friends. Some of us think our way is the only way. I'm making a suggestion to you according to the way that I do things. This is like me coming to your house and telling you how you ought to do things. You should do it this way. There's going to be a conflict. So, don't come to my Antioch, where I've got freedom and liberty, and I won't come to your Jerusalem and kick over your table. We must be respectful of other people's way of doing things.

If you choose to do that, the way you raise your children, that's your Jerusalem. The way I raise my children, that's my Antioch. I'm not going to infringe on your Jerusalem if you don't infringe on my Antioch.

Consider means to understand. We need to get an understanding that I respect whatever it is you choose to do with you, and you should respect whatever it is I choose to do with me. If it is not affecting you, if you like it, I love it. But when we are in a relationship with one another, we must find common ground. Then I can say, *"Yes, that's the way you do it. But that's not the way I do it."* You may wash dishes, and you keep the water running. I don't do it like that. You may wash the clothes and then you pile everything up

How to Have a Good Argument

in the living room. I don't do it like that. That's the way you do it. That's fine. You may go and vacuum and then dust. That's not the way I want to do it. I might cut my grass diagonally. You might cut yours horizontally. That's not the way I want to do it. Humble yourself and consider that you do not know everything about everything. Somebody else may have more information than you do and as long as it gets done, what's the big deal? There may be some more information out there that you don't have and if you go off half-cocked, there's going to be a conflict.

Secondly, you have got to confront it to conquer it. You will never conquer what you choose not to confront. Once you have properly assessed the information provided, then you are equipped to have a conversation about what is bothering you. Look at what Paul said, *"But when Peter was come to Antioch, I withstood him to the face, because he was to be blamed. For before that certain came from James, he didn't eat with the Gentiles."* Old Peter, the Jew among all Jews, was maybe sitting there eating a pork chop sandwich with the Gentiles because he said, *"Y'all sure got that smelling good."* So, he went over there and got him a sandwich. He was sitting down and then he saw some of his Jewish brothers come around the corner. and he immediately pushed the sandwich across the table and moved away from it.

Have you ever dealt with somebody who was two-faced? One minute they're this way, the next minute they are another way and you don't know who is going to show up. Peter, we're talking about the rock, this Petros, the Cephas, we're talking about him who said, *"Thou art the Christ, the son of the living God"* (Matthew 16:16). He was raised a Jew, sitting with the Gentiles, chilling until some of his friends showed up. *"Now you act like you don't have anything to do with us. Don't be acting like you didn't have a sandwich. I still see mustard in the corner of your mouth."* Paul had to confront it.

The Pastor's Pen

In the book, *Seven Habits of Highly Effective People*, Stephen Covey said, *"In Habit 5, seek first to understand, then to be understood."* He said, *"Don't go trying to get somebody to come to your side without first understanding theirs."* In other words, walk a mile in somebody else's shoes. You don't know what that sister had to go through. You don't know how she was raised up. You don't know the difficulties that she had to push through. You don't know what that man endured in his life. Because you may not know, look to understand. He watched Peter.

Now you know if he changes his habits, you start asking questions. Why? Because you made an observation. That's a different cologne than you use. What's going on? Something doesn't smell right. You never smelled that smell before. What are you doing? Seeking to understand. Why? Because if I understand, then I can be understood.

Joshua confronted Jericho because he knew he couldn't go talking about he prayed about it. You have got to put some action and feet on your faith. Yes, I'm praying about it, but I'm also going to confront it.

So, I know he is cute, but he's five years old and cussing. You better confront it. There are some things you had better confront now because when he gets fifteen, it's too late. Now is not the time to take him to the Pastor saying do something with him. It was your responsibility to confront it when it started. Do you think the Pastor is going to be able to do something in 15 minutes with you did not confront in 15 years?

Samson had to confront the Philistines. He couldn't sit back. No, he said, *"Let me get my jawbone and I'm going out here and confront."* Gideon had to confront the Midianites; he took what he had. He and his 300 went forth and conquered, but he had to confront them first. Jesus had to confront the

How to Have a Good Argument

Pharisees and the Sadducees and even confront the cross. He had to go to Jerusalem when he knew what was waiting on him in Jerusalem. He knew he had to confront it. So, what you've been putting off, you're going to have to confront. If that's your daughter, if it's your son, if it's your grandson, you are going to have to confront it. If it's your boo, or even if it's you, sometimes we need to confront ourselves. Issues will not resolve themselves.

I like what Paul said when he was concerned about Peter. He said, *"I withstood him to his face."* He didn't withstand him to his back nor did he withstand him to other believers; he withstood him to his face. Sometimes we are cowardly and we don't want to come to somebody we have a problem with and address it head on. Many of us can be passive aggressive. You know, not answering a call because you have got a problem with him or trying to get other people on your side against them when you say, *"You know what they did to me."* You want them to be angry like you are angry, and they don't even know them. Paul demonstrated that he was not that kind of man. I'm coming right to you, Peter. So, whoever the Peter or Patricia is in your life, you need to confront them. He confronted Peter to his face. Why? Because he was to be blamed.

So, what is Peter doing? It says in verses 12-13, *"For before that certain came from James, he did eat with the Gentiles: but when they were come, he withdrew and separated himself, fearing them which were of the circumcision. And the other Jews dissembled likewise with him; insomuch that Barnabas also was carried away with their dissimulation."*

What is dissimulation? It's the wearing of a mask. It's the wearing of pretense. It's fake and it's phony. It's saying one thing and doing another. Be careful with dissimulation because it will affect other people. The Apostle Paul is sharing that dissimulation is you asking people to do what you don't even do. So, it's hypocrisy. It's you, preaching, teaching, and telling folks you know, you don't need to do that, that's sin and you go out and practice the same thing. You say homosexuals are on their way to hell, but you're fornicating. This is dissimulation.

The Apostle Paul says that's dissimilation. It's phony and it's a mask. He says but Peter was also a people pleaser. What do you mean he was a people pleaser? He was a people pleaser because he was in Antioch trying to please Jerusalem. An example of this is a man that has a wife and a baby mama and you are trying to keep the peace. You're conflicted because she has opinions and she is not even in your house, and it appears that she is running your house. Here you are trying to appease the outside and appease the inside. And brother, if you are being pulled in two different directions, there is going to be some tension right up in the middle. I wonder how many have tried it and found that you can't satisfy everybody. So, you might as well satisfy the one you with. Love the one you're with. You can't do it. What will happen is you're going to alienate your wife while you're trying to appease your baby mama. Conflict will arise and your wife will get upset with you saying, *"How can you let her run this house when you said you were the man of the house?"*

It's not your weekend and you have plans with your wife and then all of a sudden ding dong. You open the door and your babies are standing there with a snotty nose, saying, *"Hey. Daddy."* So, what are you going to do? We have plans. Well, baby you know…No, no, no…you better confront that because you will never conquer that if you don't confront that. You've got to say, *"No, we have plans. I love my children, but you will not manipulate me into being submissive unto you and your way."*

How to Have a Good Argument

When you confront, stay calm. You've got to pray, and you must stay calm. A soft answer turns away wrath. Respond in a calm and peaceful manner, *"Hey, how are you doing? It's a wonderful day. The Lord is good. His mercy is everlasting. His truth endures to all."* They may get upset and say something like, *"Don't pray for me."* But kindly confront the situation at hand and go about your business. As you're walking away, they could start to shout, *"Where are you headed?"* Simply respond, *"Antioch,"* as you stay calm.

Volume and tone play a key component during a conflict. Sometimes with the people we say we love are the ones we use the wrong tone with the most. Your wife gets upset with you because of your tone. I was trying to be calm, but you talk too much. Then you start talking through your teeth saying, *"You're getting on my last nerve."* You're in there in the kitchen mumbling under your breath, *"I don't know who she thinks she is talking to."* You are angry. So, instead of you using your words and communicating, now it's all in your body language. And then when you do say something, everything is confrontational. We can't even be civil to one another.

The next thing we need to remember is to stay current. Some of us are good at recalling the past. *"See, I remember what you did, when you were standing over there by the refrigerator and you said this about my mama, you were wearing that blue shirt, and you had on them old run over shoes."* I mean, we are good at dredging up the past, so stay current. If you didn't deal with that then, don't try to deal with it now; that was is another issue. Let's deal with the current issue.

Exercise active listening. Sometimes when someone else is speaking and you say you are listening, you're really not listening; you are just waiting on your opportunity to unload.

The Pastor's Pen

Don't ever say, *"You always do…"* nor should you say, *"You never do…"* Just say, *"When you did this, I felt this way."*

Effectively communicate your feelings. If you want somebody to respect how you feel, then express how you feel. Don't expect somebody to read your mind and don't try to manipulate. You know how we do sometimes; you just say out loud what you are thinking, wanting them to pick up on it, so they'll do what you want. This is a form of manipulation.

Don't accuse; present proof. What do you mean? We see in verses 11-12, where Paul says, *"I watched you."* Here's the proof. You can't tell me you didn't do it. Let me embellish the scripture a bit to emphasis my point. Paul said something like this, *"You were sitting over there with them and then I saw your face when your homeboy showed up from Jerusalem. I saw the sandwich you were eating. How you pushed it away and you had a beer. You are doing everything now you're in Antioch, and what happens in Antioch, stays in Antioch until Jerusalem shows up."* Consider that you don't know at all. Confront to conquer.

Next, we have to vaccinate before they contaminate because if you don't, innocent bystanders will be affected. We see here in verse 13, *"And the other Jews dissembled likewise with him; insomuch that Barnabas also was carried away with their dissimulation."* Sometimes Barnabas is supposed to be the leader among leaders. We believe that he's mature enough not to succumb to dissimulation. But because it was allowed to go for a season unchecked, it becomes like wildfire. If you have got one rebellious child, and you don't check it, that weed is going to start springing up in your other children. It wasn't checked with June Bug and your other child will say, *"Why can't I do it? June Bug got to do it."* No, no you have got to deal with it because if you don't, it's going to spread and contaminate others.

How to Have a Good Argument

Leaders need to be mindful of everything they do because if they don't, they run the chance of contaminating their flock. When leaders are guilty, they need to understand that others are watching and gleaning from them.

As a Pastor, if you see me out and I got three beers in front of me, someone may say, *"I saw Pastor at Sullivans, and he had a steak, but there were three beers out there. I don't know if he and Lady were sharing, but I just saw three beers on the table and Pastor was talking all loud."* My actions may contaminate my flock or even appear to contaminate, so as a leader, I need to deny myself for the greater good of the flock because they might lose confidence in me. That's why I can say, *"It's okay for you, but what's okay for you is not okay for me."* It may not be fair, but it is to whom much is given, much is required. I can't do it, and I'm not upset about it. But if somebody sees me doing something that is perceived to be wrong and they are struggling, they may say, "Well, I saw Pastor do it, so I'm going to go ahead and do it." They end up succumbing to the pressures of it. Guess who's to blame? Me. I don't want to have to answer to God because I made somebody else fall.

Next, we need to understand the value of public versus private. What do you mean? Look at what he said in verse 14, *"But when I saw that they walked not uprightly according to the truth of the gospel, I said unto Peter before them all…"* Now he confronted Peter privately; he said to his face. But he said, *"I saw this thing was catching on around."* So, then he said, *"I'm going to have to take this confrontation not only to this person singularly, but I'm going to have to speak to the whole group."* See, sometimes we go public with stuff that should be private. Some of us are so quick to go on social media and air dirty laundry that's some private stuff that should never have been made public. Then when your sisters get a hold of it and they start treating your boo differently, you're wondering, *"Why they got an attitude with my man, and they are just jealous."* No, you done talked him down and they are wondering why you a fool still with him. So don't talk him down in front of your sisters. Don't talk him down in front of your mama. On the flip side, don't talk her down in front of your mother by saying things like, *"She can't cook like you, Mama."* Mama might say, *"Well, that's okay."* You know what you and Mama are doing? You're throwing gas on that fire. You don't mess up that relationship because you're running your mouth. *"Shut up!"* Build her up; everything she cooks is good, her peach cobbler and everything. You have got to learn that you don't bring other folks in. Some stuff is private, and there is a difference between secrecy and privacy.

Finally, we need to remember to respond out of relationship. In verse 20, he said, *"I am crucified with Christ: nevertheless I live; yet not I, but Christ liveth in me: and the life which I now live in the flesh I live by the faith of the Son of God, who loved me, and gave himself for me."* What is he saying? I can't operate in who I used to be. He said, *"I'm operating out of my relationship with Jesus Christ."* When you engage in confrontation, remember who you are.

That takes me back to Wakanda when the king was losing the battle. I could hear his mother in the background saying, *"Show him who you are."* We have to remember who we are in Christ Jesus and when we are engaged in a confrontation, and it seems like we are about to lose. Show them who you are. Sometimes you're got to be quiet because everything doesn't warrant a response from you. I know that's hard for some of us, especially those of us of the female persuasion. Don't get angry, I'm just telling the truth because sometimes you have to say something. You could just be quiet, but that thing is eating you up and the Holy Ghost is saying, *"Shh,"* and that flesh is crying out. *"He isn't going to talk to me like that. Talking about submitting, I don't submit."* When are you going to submit? *"Hush."* Hold your peace and let the Lord fight your battle.

So, what did they do? They found compromise in verse 10. It says, *"Only they would that we should remember the poor; the same which I also was forward to do."* And Paul said, *"The same, which I was always forward to do."* He said, *"I'm doing that anyway."* But if you read Acts 15, they went a little bit more in depth. He told them to abstain from idols, from fornication, from things strangled, and from blood. So, if we're going to have good conflict resolutions, we must find an equally beneficial compromise.

Can you compromise on your stance? Is winning more important to you than the relationship? Because some of us, will not compromise. *"No, I'm right. I'm right and you're wrong."* Compromise. Find some common ground and get there and stand on it.

How can we compromise in this situation? And some of you just said in your spirit, *"Do it my way. We can compromise in this situation if you do it my way."*

I'm crucified with Christ. What does that mean? He took something from me. It means a work that was completed in the past has ongoing results. He took it away. I was crucified with Christ. It is no longer I who lives, but Christ in me. He took something from me only to give something to me. No longer me, but Him. For in Him we live, and move, and have our being; it's in Him. Without Him, I'm nothing, but through Him, all things are possible. I've got to recognize that He took it away, but He also gave me something. It's not an improved life. It's not a reformed life. It's an exchanged life. My unrighteousness for His righteousness. My weakness for His strength. My brokenness for His wholeness. My darkness for His light. He brought me out of darkness into the marvelous light. Why? Because I'm crucified with Him.

The Pastor's Pen

And it says, *"I'm crucified with Him,"* but He says, *"He loved me and gave Himself for me."*

Those are two truths you and I need to remember. He loves me. I am not always right, but He loves me. I may not be the cutest, but He loves me. I may not be the most handsome, but He loves me. You may not be the prettiest, but He loves you. You've got to say, *"I'm not as slim as I used to be, but He loves me. I may make up and mess up sometimes, but He loves me. I've overcome some hurdles, but He loves me. I fall down sometimes, but He loves me. He loves me even when I cannot fathom why."* He says, *"I love you with an undying love and you'll never be separated from the love of God in Christ Jesus."* He loves me. He loves you. He loves us and then He gave Himself for us. He gave Himself. I'm so glad that when it got hard, He didn't turn away. He confronted the situation. Sin was standing up in our faces saying, *"I got them down."* But Jesus said, *"I confront the sin. I'll put it to shame. I'll stand on it victorious."* We need to remember that we are more than conquerors through Him that loves us.

Chapter 2
Don't Eat That

Genesis 3:1-4 and 2 Kings 4:38-42

I'm reminded of Martin Luther King that in 1956, he was caught up in the midst of what would become the bus boycott. He was pastoring his first pastorate in Montgomery, Alabama; and he was doing all he could to bring forth civil rights for people that looked like him while he was operating in the midst of a racist society. While in Alabama, Rosa Parks decided *"I'm not getting out of my seat today, my feet hurt, I've been on them all day and I'm not moving."* She sat there and did not move, which was the birthing of the civil rights movement.

Through all of that, Martin was subjected to threats on his life. The phone would ring, then they'd hang up. One night, while he and his wife were sleeping in January, the phone rang in the middle of the night and he sprang out bed. Because of who he was, he had to answer it. He jumped out of bed, went to the phone, answered it and on the other end was a gruff, growling voice; the voice on the other end began to speak racial slurs and continued by saying, *"We are sick of your mess. If you are not out of town in the next three days, we are going to blow up your house with your family in it and we're going to blow your brains out."* Then the line goes dead.

Martin is gripped with fear because his wife and infant daughter were sleeping in the next room. He wonders, *"Lord, are you with me or not? I've got to admit I'm afraid."* As Martin brooded over a cup of coffee, something began to stir down on the inside of him saying, *"Stand up for righteousness, stand up for truth, stand up for peace and I will be with you always even unto the ends of the earth."* From that moment on, Martin took a step and another step and another step on his path that God had laid out for him.

He almost ate what they were trying to serve on that phone but when the Lord spoke in his spirit, He said, *"Don't eat that. I've still got a purpose. I still got a plan for your life."* I'm trying to encourage you, don't eat what the enemy is trying to tell you. The enemy is good at telling us that this or that will never happen or never occur, but we have to learn to trust God at His word. God will tell us, *"I still got a purpose for you. I've still got a plan for your life. Don't eat that because he wants you to get distracted and he wants you to believe the lie."* God knows the facts, so instead of believing the lies, trust the truth.

The doctor may have given you a diagnosis, but God, believe that He's everything to you and He's still life and breath. He's still a healer. He's still my peace. He's still my master. I'm not going to eat anything that contradicts what I know about my God.

In this chapter that we're reading in 2 Kings 4, there are a few nuggets we can glean from before we get to the meat of the message. First, it gives us the poor widow, you remember her, her husband had died, and she said, *"I don't have anything in the house but a pot of oil."* The Lord instructed her to go borrow some vessels. Essentially, He was saying, *"Go get in some more debt."* You know that's how God works. He'll instruct you to do something that just doesn't make sense. Get in some more debt, then I'm going to save you. So, she went and borrowed the vessels. She had told the man of God that she didn't have but a little oil, and she was instructed to pour it out and it kept pouring until she didn't have any more vessels to fill. I'm just trying let somebody who thought they didn't have nothing, God said, *"If you got a little something, I can stretch it, if you trust me."*

In this scripture, not only do we encounter the poor widow, but there's a prominent woman, the rich Shunammite woman. The man of God said, *"What can I do for you?"* She said, *"I'm good. I got my own people. I got my own money. I got my own honey, I'm good."* And then Elijah said to his servant, *"What can I do for her?"* He said, *"Her husband is old and she doesn't have any children."* Elisha knew what to do and began to speak to her saying, *"By this time next year, you are going hold a child, a son even."* And she said, *"Wait a minute, my Lord, don't lie to me; my husband is old."* Elijah held fast onto his word and said, *"Like I said by this time next year, you are going to hold the son."* And it came to pass that by that time next year, she held the son. That means something happened in the old man. You can see where I'm going with this.

Satisfying a Legitimate Need in an Illegitimate Way

We see where God takes us to the prophet's wilderness. The enemy wants to convince you to satisfy a legitimate need in an illegitimate way. Hunger is a natural thing, but you have to know how to satisfy your hunger. Have you ever just been hungry and you eat anything? You just open the refrigerator and you just eat anything. You're eating sardines and crackers; you're making a peanut butter sandwich. None of that goes together, but you are just trying to fill the empty place. Not only is that true naturally, but it becomes true spiritually because many times we have an empty space within us and it's not filled with anything, so we're doing anything and everything to try to fill that empty space. I'm trying to tell somebody; everything that looks good isn't good for you.

When we look at where they are in Gilgal, they are in the midst of a famine, a dry place. There's nothing flowing, nothing 's operating, and the Bible says, *"When they get there, they are seated at the feet of the man of God."*

Let's walk through this because I don't want you to think I've just made this up. No, this is in the word of God. God provided context for the man and the woman in the garden, for which he had provided for them. He said, *"This is your stew, the place where I have provided for you,"* and they chose to receive their sustenance outside of the context of what God had provided. God said, *"You can eat out of any of these trees."* There was a multitude of trees they could have eaten from, but they wanted what God said no to. Just like us, we want the very things God tells us we cannot have. We say, *"I'm big and bad enough. It might have hurt somebody, but it isn't going to hurt me."* You are going to destroy your life. You've got to determine in your heart and mind that, *"Lord, for You I live, and for You I'll die."*

Let's go to Isaiah 51:3, *"For the Lord shall comfort Zion: he will comfort all her waste places; and he will make her wilderness like Eden, and her desert like the garden of the Lord; joy and gladness shall be found therein, thanksgiving, and the voice of melody."* What is he saying?

Don't Eat That

The transformative power of the word of God shall change your waste places into places of plenty. But many times, we are not operating in the word of God. We are not operating within the context of what God has provided because we want to operate in our reasoning. And then we find ourselves in the wilderness, in a dry place, in an empty space and we're trying to fill it with everything except for the word of God.

He says in Deuteronomy 30:19, *"I call heaven and earth to record this day against you, that I have set before you life and death, blessing and cursing: therefore choose life, that both thou and thy seed may live."* He said, *"If you choose life every day, you have a faith choice."* You're either going to choose what God said, or you're going to choose what you feel. So, if you choose what you feel, guess what? You have chosen death. You may not physically die because you made the wrong choice, but it means things that you are connected to will begin to die. You have to say, *"Lord, I want life around me, so I'm going to dwell in that which is life. Your word is life."*

The enemy wants to convince you to satisfy a legitimate need in an illegitimate way. You are not going to die. That's the first thing he'll tell you. So, you've got to decide, *"What am I going to choose? Am I going to choose spirit, or am I going to choose flesh? Am I going to choose life, or am I going to choose death?"*

What Do We Do in the Crisis?

Let's move on to number two. It's about what we do in the crisis. The scripture tells how Elijah came unto Gilgal and there was a dearth (famine) in the land and the sons of the prophets were sitting at the feet of Elijah. Wait a minute. . . you mean to tell me they are having church in the wilderness? What is Elijah sharing with them? Was he sharing the first five books of the Bible: Genesis, Exodus,

The Pastor's Pen

Leviticus, Numbers, and Deuteronomy? He was sharing from the word of God. They're in a famine and he's sharing the Word. In today's world, when something isn't going right, people run from the church, but as we see in this scripture, things weren't right and they ran to the church. When you come to the church, you are going to get a word from God that will transform your life. You got to say, "*Lord, I need a word today. I didn't come to play. I didn't come to see what you were wearing; I didn't come to see what kind of hat you got on, but I came because I need a word from God.*" So, when you step into the sanctuary, you're praying to God and trusting that He will give the pastor a word that will answer your questions, speak to your situation, and bring peace to the situation you're facing. You need a word that's going to help you through this valley that you're in and help you through this wilderness you're in. You're seeking help so that He will transform this famine into a place of plenty, and you know it will only come through a word from God.

What do you do in a crisis? Notice where they are; the Bible says Gilgal. We first learned of Gilgal in Joshua 5:9. They went to this place after Moses' death and Joshua has taken over. We're in chapter five where they are preparing to circumcise the people as the Lord instructed. They needed to get some sharp knives. They asked, "*Why, Lord, do you need to circumcise the children a second time?*" He answered and said, "*They still got some flesh. They've been walking with me for forty years, but they still got some flesh that needs to be removed.*" Spiritually, we can be walking with God and still have some flesh. So, God says, "*I need you to go to Gilgal because Gilgal means the rolling place, the rolling away of the reproach, the rolling away of the shame. This is the place where you go, so I can take off of you that which time has put upon you.*"

Don't Eat That

I know what your mama said about you. I know what your daddy said. I know what the generational curse says, but God said, *"This is Gilgal; this is the place I'm cutting away some stuff from you that the enemy has tried to put on you."* You didn't even know why you were so thirsty for alcohol, but it was some generational curse that was in your family that came down upon you. You didn't know why you lusted after this or lusted after that, but it was a generational curse, and your cousin walked in it and now you've got to say, *"I'm at Gilgal now and that stuff has got to roll away."*

What's amazing? They were Gilgal, but it was still a famine. You say, *"God, I'm spiritually in a higher place than I've ever been before, but when I look around, I'm in a famine."* How is it that you can be in a famine, but God is working on you? I just wonder how many of you have ever said, *"God is working in my life. I feel the anointing that is upon me, but God, I'm in a famine."* God says, *"Don't look at your circumstance, because your life is in you. If My word is in you, life is in you."*

This is a rolling place. They are in a famine, but they choose to sit down and hear a word. My heart may be broken, but sit down and hear a word. You might not have your spouse, but sit down and hear a word from the Lord. Things might not look the way you want them to look; you may not be driving the car you want to drive or living in the house you want to live in, but I dare you to sit down and hear ye the word of the Lord. They were in a famine and went to church. They were starving, but they stopped to hear the word. My stomach is growling, but I need a word from the Lord. They shall no longer hunger nor thirst, but they shall be filled. We need to remember that the Old Testament is the New Testament concealed, but the New Testament is the Old Testament revealed. You got to tell the Lord, *"Thank you for filling my empty place."*

The Pastor's Pen

You know what they were doing. . .they didn't let the famine dominate their attention. Some of us are easily swayed and use small things to keep us from church. Oh, they're talking crazy on my job; I don't feel like going to church. So, you're huffing and puffing, and you aren't ever going to get above that thing because you have eaten from the wrong table. You got to say, *"Wait a minute. God gave me this job. Who cares? If God be for me, who can be against me?"* Where is the word that will spring up in you in famine? You've got to say, *"God is for me and nobody can be against me."* Now make sure you are doing what you are supposed to be doing. Don't be at work on Facebook when you're supposed to be working; do your work. Because if you're fired, then you'll come to church fussing at the pastor saying, *"Pastor, you told me the Lord was on my side and I still got fired."* Yeah, if you're doing right.

I'm not going to let this dominate my attention. I'm going to stay focused on the word of the Lord. What did Jesus say? He said, *"Man shall not live by bread alone, but by every word that comes out of the mouth of God."* I'm listening to what God has to say; I'm trying to hear what God has to say. I know what circumstances are saying. I know what they're saying in the White House, but what does God have to say? We won't know until we sit and hear a word from God. We've got to get a word from the Lord.

The system of this world is in a freefall of famine. You have to determine that system is not what I'm living my life according to. I'm living my life according to the word of God. Matthew 6:33 says, *"Seek ye first the Kingdom of God and his righteousness and all these other things will be added."* I have to get in His word. My decisions need to be filtered through His word. My words need to be filtered through His word. How I'm going to act and react needs to be filtered through His word.

Don't Eat That

Listen to what it says in Psalm 119:130, *"The entrance of thy words giveth light; it giveth understanding unto the simple."* You don't know what to do. You don't know how to do it. Get in His word, and He said His word will give you light. What is light? See, darkness is ignorance. No knowledge. I went to bed and I didn't know, but I woke up and I did know. God can do amazing things you need to know and believe that God can speak to you while you're sleeping. You do know when your natural body is sleeping, your spirit is wide awake. So, God says that what He can do is make a deposit in your spirit that you won't be privy to until you're conscious again, and all of a sudden you say, I know what to do, when to do it, and how to do it, because I got into His word and His word got into me.

His word will give you some light. Then it says, *"His word will give you understanding."* Yeah, that's when David said, *"When I made it to the sanctuary, then I understood therein."* He said that it was in the sanctuary that he understood some things because the word was in the sanctuary.

Be Careful Who You Allow to Add to Your Stew

There was dearth in the land, and the sons of the prophets were sitting before him. He said unto his servants, *"Sit on the great pot."* Wait a minute. It's a famine. Notice, teaching came before the supernatural. Teaching precedes the supernatural. Jesus never did a supernatural act without first doing some teaching. Let me just give you one example in Luke 5, Peter was by the seaside, and he had been fishing all night and caught nothing. After catching nothing, he was washing his nets and giving up. As they were doing this Jesus desired to borrow Peter's boat and took the boat, and from the boat He taught the people. Then after He finished teaching, He said, *"Peter, launch out into the deep for a catch of fish."* Wait a minute, you mean, tell me, Master, Savior Jesus, we toiled all night and there aren't any more fish. It's daylight, and this isn't even the right time to go fishing. Jesus said, *"What did I say?"* Peter said, *"But nevertheless at your word."* Jesus said, *"Cast your nets."* Read your Bible carefully and pay close attention because if we read it too quickly, we will miss it. Peter replied, *"At your word, I'll drop the net."* Do you see that? Jesus instructed him to drop his nets, plural; while Peter spoke in the singular, one net. So, he was partially obedient, and the Bible tells us that as soon as he dropped that one little net, all of a sudden, the net was overflowing with fish. We see where teaching preceded the supernatural. God says, *"If we ever get ahold of teaching instead of being entertained, something is going to happen in our lives."* So, I have to be careful who I allow to add to my stew because not everybody is a cook.

They were sitting before him and they were in a famine and the man of God said, *"Now after you have been taught, put on the pot."* Let's look at the situation a little closer. We're hungry, there isn't any food around here, but the man of God said, *"Put on the pot."* I'm trying to get someone's attention. It's been dry, but God said, *"Put on the pot."* May not have what you want, but put on the pot. What are you saying? Put on the pot of your belief and believe God for what you want to put in your pot. God. You say, *"I'm believing that You're able to do exceedingly abundantly above all I can ask or think."* He said, *"Put on the pot."* We see here the first recorded potluck; there was a church service, and after the service, they ate.

Wait a minute. In 2 Kings 4:38, we see where he told his servant, Gehazi to set on the great pottage for the sons of the prophets, and one went out. Who are you? I didn't ask you to do anything, but here we are being overzealous. We want to help. So, one went out into the field to gather herbs and found a wild vine. He gathered three of those wild gourds and shredded them into the pot of pottage, for they knew not. They didn't know where stuff came from.

Do you know that when you are operating in your pot, there's always somebody trying to sow a wild vine in it? You start talking about what God is going to do, and they are going to say, *"Now you know God gave you five senses, and I know you don't believe all that stuff they be talking about down there at that church. You don't have any business going down there all the time; why do you go there every week? What are you doing? You giving them your money? What is wrong with you?"* They are trying to sow a wild vine in your stew. You've got to say, *"Wait a minute."* While putting your hand over your pot, you say, *"No, I'm not listening."*

Ephesians 1:3 says, *"Blessed be the God and Father of our Lord Jesus Christ, who hath blessed us with all spiritual blessings in heavenly places in Christ."* I've got what I need, and it's already done, and it's in Christ in heavenly places. The way you get it out of the heavenly places into your life can only be done by faith. Do you believe that?

Let's look at Matthew 9:20-21, *"And, behold, a woman, which was diseased with an issue of blood twelve years, came behind him, and touched the hem of his garment: For she said within herself, If I may but touch his garment, I shall be whole."* What is she doing? She is putting a demand on the one who can give it to her. It was already around her, but she had to put a demand on it to draw it down out of the heavenly places through her faith. So, she kept saying to herself, *"I'm to be made whole. Now it's been twelve years. It didn't work for twelve years. I sought all the physicians. I spent all my money. I tried everything, but I haven't tried this yet, but I'm just believing that He's able to do it, so I'm going to keep saying to myself I'm going to be made whole. I'm going to be made whole if I can touch but the hem of His garment. I'm going to be made whole.*" She didn't touch Him. Her faith was strong enough to believe that she only needed to touch what's on Him. Where is your faith? Stop allowing the negative talk, even if it's your own talk, deny you what God has already given unto you. I'm trying to awaken you. I'm shaking you, wake up!

Your faith has been asleep and you're just letting it sleep. You're slumbering and the alarm clock went off a long time ago. You just keep sleeping, but it's time to wake up.

Notice the man of God initiated the stew, now here comes some trainee. He decided on his own that he was going to put something in this pot because this isn't good. Let me help you.

This mindset is the reason why pastors and church leaders can't let everybody come to the church and preach and teach. It's a wild vine. People have called me saying, "*I got a word for your people.*" "*No, you don't. The Lord gave me a word and guess what? I'm going to deliver it if the Lord allows me.*" I have to be tuned into the voice of God in order to discern as the shepherd of the flock God has given me. I can't allow just anyone to come that says, "*I have a word.*" Unfortunately, most of it is not so they can share a word, but so they can get an honorarium.

You aren't going to put a wild vine in my stew and have folks confused. Just because you mean well doesn't mean it is going to end well. Man, don't let that woman give you a wild vine. Woman, don't let that man give you a wild vine. The Bible says, "*If it's not of faith, it is sin.*"

Here you are trying to operate by faith, and you turn on that news. The economy is down. Food prices are high. Gas prices are high. You know your bills are going up, but I'm not getting an increase on my Social Security. You got to understand we are not of this system; God is always operating on our behalf.

The prices are going up. There are wars and rumors of wars. People are starving, People are sick. People are tired; people are sick and tired. There's division. There's racism. There's malice. There's strife. There's envy. You're letting it get in your stew. It will fizzle out the flame of your faith. And you'll start operating according to reason instead of in the supernatural realm where God wants you to be.

You do know there weren't any fish, but when he threw that net in, all of a sudden fish were in the net in the daytime. And the fish could see the net, but they swam right in it. Why? Because God says, *"You're operating in the supernatural, and when you operate in the supernatural, what you desire will come to you."* That's why you've got to be careful what you say. My wife always says, *"Don't you say it because everything you say comes to pass."*

I have to be careful when I see somebody hanging around my daughter I don't like. I say, *"Lord, as far as the east is from the west, separate their footsteps, Jesus."* Then I'll be looking for that little boy, where is so and so? The Bible says, *"You'll look for them, but you won't be able to find them."*

So, what do we have? We got seeds. We got trees. We got deeds. You do know that the word of God is a seed. Let's look at 1 Peter 1:23, *"Being born again, not of corruptible seed, but of incorruptible, by the word of God, which liveth and abideth for ever."*

See, a lot of people think born again just means one time. He said, *"The more you get into this word, the more you're born again."* It's transformative. My mind has been transformed and I don't think like I used to think. I don't say what I used to say. I don't go where I used to go. I don't play how I used to play. Why? Because the Word is changing me. You start thinking better. You start thinking differently. You see things differently. You see people differently. So, He says, "*I need to put a seed in you.*" You must realize that a seed has to be sown before it can grow. In Mark 4:28-29, it says, "*Every seed once you planted it produces after its own kind. Then it puts forth the blade, then the ear, then the full grain in the ear.*" What am I saying? Every seed has progressive results. Some of us are at blade, some at ear, and some of us are at full grain in the ear, meaning that God is saying to us, "*You ought to be a whole lot further along then you used to be.*" It's progressive.

Psalm 1:2-3, "*But his delight is in the law of the Lord; and in his law doth he meditate day and night...*" Meditation is saying that scripture over and over and over in your spirit. That's what that woman with the issue of blood was doing. She was meditating and upon meditation, it brought manifestation. When I meditated on it, it became a part of my life. It healed me from the inside out.

In Psalm 1:3 it says, "*And he shall be like a tree planted by the rivers of water, that bringeth forth his fruit in his season; his leaf also shall not wither; and whatsoever he doeth shall prosper.*" Now let's talk about the tree. A tree can be of good seed, and it can be of bad seed. An oak tree was just once upon a time just one acorn. But now it's a mighty oak tree standing, providing shade, swaying in the wind because it's rooted and grounded; the winds blow, but it doesn't blow over.

If you get a negative tree growing up in you, it's hard to remove. So, if you keep eating that seed of negativity, you're going to bring forth a tree that will produce the fruit of negativity in your life. That's why some of you right now rolling your eyes instead of rejoicing over the word that God is trying to get to you. You've got to be able to say, "*Lord, let me receive this so that my life can be transformed by what You're saying."* Whatever that is in your life is the direct result of the seed you've been eating. As we think in our hearts, so are we.

You have seen those giant sequoias and giant redwoods trees in California, trees where they have cut a hole in, and you can drive a car through it. Huge trees. So, what if that is a negative tree that's in your spirit big enough to drive a truck through. How dark is that darkness? You've got to say, *"Lord, anything that's not like You, I want it uprooted out of my life so that I can walk in the liberty that is in Christ Jesus. I need Your word."* Job trusted the word of God and knew it was as necessary as food. So, when Job was going through turbulent times and on the emotional roller coaster, he said, *"Thy word is my necessary food."*

Not only were there seeds and trees, but there were deeds. Elijah didn't care what the season declared. He said, *"Put the pot on."* I dare you to put the pot on in the midst of a famine and believe God. The job may downsize and your job will be included, but I dare you to put the pot on and remain faithful while you confess, *"My God shall supply all of my needs according to his riches in glory."*

Discernment Brings Deliverance

Look at what he says in 2 Kings 4:40, *"So they poured out for the men to eat. And it came to pass, as they were eating of the pottage, that they cried out, and said, O thou man of God, there is death in the pot..."* It says they cried out; it didn't say they died. It said they cried. Sometimes you have to be able to discern. When they roll up on you and you can tell you know, they're fake. You know, they don't mean you any good, but you got to be able to say, *"Praise the Lord, God bless you."* Then send them on their way in Jesus' name. You've got to know when there's some death in the pot.

They're trying to be as genuine looking as they can, but sometimes God will put a check in your spirit. You need to recognize the devil and remind him that he isn't anything but a phony. You are a hypocrite of all hypocrites. You are from your father, the devil. You don't have to say it to them. You can be saying it in your spirit because some folks will look at you and think you're crazy.

Man of God, there is death in the pot. It doesn't say they died, but somebody discerned death. The whole pot of stew, the stew was good, but one little wild vine messed up the whole thing. Jesus said, *"A little leaven will leaven the whole lump."* He's trying to tell you that you don't have to get a whole lot of poison in your pot; a little bit of poison can take you out.

Counteract the Contradiction

I can't eat. I can't put it in my pot because there's death in it. What must I do? You must counteract the contradiction. Let's go back to 2 Kings 4:41, *"But he said, Then bring meal. And he cast it into the pot; and he said, Pour out for the people, that they may eat. And there was no harm in the pot."* It says, *"But he said."* Before the "but," there was death in the pot; after the "but," everybody is eating and full. I just wonder if there's anybody that believes Psalm 30:5, *"For his anger endureth but a moment; in his favour is life: weeping may endure for a night, but joy cometh in the morning."* It's probable and possible that weeping will endure, but it is definitely going to happen that joy is coming. It's a promise that joy is coming in the morning. Luke 5:32 says, *"I came not to call the righteous, but sinners to repentance."* He says, *"If you think you are well and you think you've got it all going on, then I didn't come for you."* He said, *"I come for those that are broken and contrite, knowing that they can't*

Don't Eat That

do it without Me. Lord, without You, I can do nothing but through You all things are possible."

Romans 12:21, *"Be not overcome of evil, but overcome evil with good."* That does something for your vindictive spirit. When you want to get even with people instead of just saying, *"I'm going to let God handle that and I'm going to overcome evil with good."* So, when you go to work tomorrow, buy lunch for the one that gets on your nerves. I can hear you now in the spirit saying, *"I'm not buying them lunch. You've got to be crazy."* You're operating in another realm. So do what is not expected, buy them lunch. In Matthew 24:35, it says, *"Heaven and earth shall pass away, but my word shall never pass away."*

Notice the scripture says, *"But he said, Then bring meal."* Then bring meal is capitalized. Bring meal. It's like he was saying, *"Since you're dealing with this, then do this."* Do you know where meal comes from? It comes from a seed. We're right back where we were. I'm trying to show you something. When you know you've got some poison trying to be put in your pot, the way to counteract the contradiction in your pot is to put more seed. He said, *"Put some meal on it."* Let me see if you can guess if you can receive this. On that Franks Hot Sauce commercial, they say they put it on everything. Put some meal on it. I put that on everything. On my sons, I put that meal on him. On my daughter, I put the meal on her. On my home, I put the meal on it. At my job, I put the meal on it. In the church, I put the meal on it. I put that on everything. He capitalized it. Why? Because it's important. Because after he put that meal in there, the Bible says, *"And there was no harm."* I know what the doctor said he saw on the scan, but God says, *"If you go on and put this word on it, there will be no harm."*

I'm just trying to encourage somebody. I know what it looked like on the job, but if you put some meal on it, my God shall supply all of your needs according to His riches in glory. What am I doing? I'm putting some meal on it. I'm not going to react the way you desire for me to react. I'm not going to panic. I'm not going to run and hide. I'm going to put some meal on it so that I can walk in what God called me to walk in. I'm going to walk in deliverance. I'm going to walk in healing. I'm going to walk in victory because I put some meal on it.

You do know we were in the Garden of Eden, and we let somebody sow a wild vine. And here we are in that wild vine, overcome with sin. But God sent His son. Who is His son? He is the bread of life. He's the meal that the Lord said, *"I'm going to sprinkle some meal on this and there won't be no harm."* I'm no longer a sinner; I've been overcome. He said, *"I've delivered you from the penalty of sin, from the power of sin and now every day I'm being delivered from the practice of sin."* Why? Because greater is He that is in me, then he that is in the world. He has sprinkled the meal on me.

Chapter 3
A Change is Coming

Luke 24:50-53

James Baldwin said it this way, "*Not everything that is faced can be changed, but nothing can be changed until it is faced.*" Deepak Chopra said, "*All great changes are preceded by great chaos.*" I'm trying to get someone to understand that if you're dealing with some chaos, God is sending some change.

There was a man seated at his desk and he had been busy at work all day. He had stuff all over his desk and was working hard trying to make a dollar out of 15 cents. Then he noticed an envelope on his desk and opened it. To his dismay and surprise, it was a termination letter. He had given the company 25 years of his life. He started when he was 35. He says to himself, "*I'm going to lose my house. I'm going to have to drastically change my lifestyle.*" He sat dejected and in despair and could feel the weight of depression creeping in on him. Inadvertently, he saw a spider sitting on his desk and he swung to sweep it off out of frustration. He watched the spider as it excreted a thread from its body and gently let itself down to the floor. He started thinking, *"If this creature can react to change from something that is within him, how is it that I'm worried when I know greater is He that is in me than he that is in the world? Why is it that I have forgotten about the greatness that is within me which is not affected by what's going on around me? Yes, I may lose this job, but God can give me another job. What I have to do is make sure I don't lose my mind because I'm going to need my mind for the next job God gives me."*

We need to learn that change is inevitable, but it doesn't have to be incapacitating. We are not stopped or stalled just because some change has happened in our lives. As a matter of fact, change is the only constant in life because if you look at yourself today and you look at yourself from 15 years ago, you would say, "Oh, what a change." I don't care how many filters you put on your picture; oh, what a change. What else can we learn?

When change rushes in, how you respond to the change will determine the level of your survival. That's why you can't be worried about who's in the White House. That's in a constant state of flux. It's constantly changing. Mental statuses are constantly plummeting. We have to know that they are human just like we are, so we have to look higher. Set your sights on things above and not on things around you. Keep your focus on Jesus.

God has given you what you need on the inside to meet your situation on the outside. This change is saying goodbye to one thing and hello to something new. Sometimes we're so busy looking back that we don't see that God is giving us something new right in front of us. Here we are pining over what was lost and pining over who was lost when God says in Isaiah 43:18-19, *"I've got something new."* He said, *"Fret*

A Change is Coming

not for the things of old, neither consider them behold, I do a new thing." I don't know about you, but I'm looking for God to do something new.

Luke closes his gospel the same way he started it. He started it with a priest named Zacharias. And here, he ends it with the high priest named Jesus. He closes with the ascension of Christ and begins with the birthing of Christ. It's something when you think about the books of the Bible and how God unfolds the mystery unto us. Every page we turn, He's showing us something new about the Savior. When we look at this end of it, it is the closing of His earthly ministry, but it's the beginning of His heavenly ministry. He's closing where He's healed, He's delivered, He's set free, and He's made whole, but He's opening His intercession ministry. He's seated at the right hand of the Father interceding for you and me. I don't know about you, but sometimes I need somebody to pray for me. And when I can't get you to pray, Jesus said, *"Don't worry, I'm always up. I never sleep, nor do I slumber. I'm always on the throne for you."* And somebody needed Him to pray last night. It's the curtain call; it's the consummation of His mission. He came to save the world from their sin.

The Lord told me to tell you, *"I have left so that they can bear witness of My mission in the earth, that you ought to tell others that there is a Savior and His name is Jesus. That He is still opening blinded eyes, that He's still opening stopped up ears. He's still regulating the tongue that has been tied by the circumstances of this life. He is still our healer and our deliverer. He's still Jehovah Rapha. He's still Jehovah Nissi. He's still Jehovah Shalom and He's still providing in the earth what we need."*

So, what benefits can we glean from the ascension of Jesus Christ?

The Pastor's Pen

He Carried the Burden

First in verse 50, the Lord said, *"Tell them that He carried the burden."* He completed the mission. Yes, some of us, we're carrying a burden this morning. I hear my Bible saying, *"Cast your cares upon Him because He cares for you."* He understands what it means to carry a heavy burden because even Him, when the heaviest burden was laid upon His shoulder, He stumbled with it and there was somebody there to help Him to carry the burden. I'd like to encourage you and let you know that there are many crosses in this life, but the Lord says, *"I'm here to help you carry your burden."* He's a burden bearer. He's a heavy load sharer.

Verse 50 said, *"And he led them out as far as to Bethany..."* He's been out of the grave for some 40 days now. This isn't the same day that He rose; this is 40 days after He was risen from the dead and here, they are spending time with Jesus. I can only imagine because I would have done it if I were there, I would have said, *"What was it like on the other side? What was it like to be put in a tomb and walk out the back door? What was it like when the light of the world was in the midst of the darkness of this world? What was it like for you to be held by death, but then death couldn't hold you?"* I just wonder what it was like. I would have been asking a few questions. *"Lord, can You just tell me where the sting of death is? Where is the victory in the grave?"* He said, *"Because I am victorious, you shall be victorious."* I just wonder what they asked Him.

John 16:12 says it this way, *"I have many things to tell you the likes of which you cannot bear right now."* I don't know about you, but I wonder. I believe that in those 40 days He was telling them many things, and I'm so glad He's still telling us many things. And in the midnight hour, He comes and He gives me many things, many things of how to deal

A Change is Coming

with the burdens of the life that we're living. Many things of how to come out of the darkness, many things of how to be strengthened in weakness, many things of how to deal with your sons and your daughters, your grandsons, your granddaughters, your wives, your husbands. He says, "*I have come that you might have a life and have it more abundantly.*" He carried the burden. He says, "*...He led them out as far as Bethany.*" It means He went as far as He could with them. It took 40 days to get to Bethany.

Let me see if I can make that a little plainer for you because my mother came to me and it was my Bethany moment. When I was 13 years old, she came to me with a very serious look on her face. I was wondering, *"What in the world have I done now?"* I'll never forget it. She said, "*Son, sit down, I got something I need to tell you.*" She looked me right in my eye and began to say, "*Your sins are no longer on me. You know better. So, therefore, you have to do better.*" When she told me that, it shook me to my core. I didn't know how to articulate what I was feeling at the moment. But I had a real sensation that God was real and one day I was going to have to stand before Him. She continued by saying, "*You've got to get yourself together because it's going to be you standing before Him and not me.*" I was only 13 years old and in essence she was saying, "*I have done my part, now it's time for you to apply it. I have brought you this far, but it's time for you to take action. I have to release you. I'm not abandoning you. I will be here to support you, but you have to step out and be mindful of your own actions.*" This was our Bethany moment.

I've gone as far as I can go with you and I wonder, where was your Bethany? Where was it that you determined, "I've gone as far as I can go?" When you had to tell your son, "*We're at Bethany now. I bent over backwards for you. I bailed you out of this and I bailed you out of that. I pulled you out of this. I pulled you out of that and now we're at*

Bethany. I've gone as far as I can go." That daughter, *"I've gone as far as I can go. I told you right from wrong, but there you are going about your own business. I'm in Bethany. I've gone as far as I can go with you."*

I know it's a tough place because the word Bethany means house of rejoicing and house of affliction. It's two extremes at the same time and every one of us has been in a situation where we've experienced joy and sorrow at the same time. I'm rejoicing because of this, but I'm kind of sad because of that. I want to go and tell somebody from the mountaintops about this, but I won't tell anybody about that. I'm in the house of Bethany and this is as far as I can go.

It's the place of impartation. It's the place where God puts something in you that you can't get from other places. They could not have gotten it from a priest in the temple. They could not have gotten it from the threshing floor. They could not have gotten it out in the field. They had to be with Jesus. Nicodemus couldn't do it. Joseph of Arimathea could not do it. There was nobody in the land that could provide what Jesus was providing when they made it to Bethany, and it was nobody but the Lord.

When they got to Bethany, they were two miles from Jerusalem. Why did the Lord pull that out for me? The Lord said, *"Tell them they're closer than they think."* See, they could look over and see the city of peace, that's what Jerusalem means. *Jeru* means *city* and *salem* means *peace*. So, He said that they could look over and see it, but they were not there yet. I'm talking to somebody that can sense they're closer than they've ever been to the breakthrough that God has for them. He told me to tell you, *"You're closer than you've ever been before. It's not just around the corner; it's nigh unto thee even at the door."* Just begin to thank Him and say, *"I'm closer. I'm closer. I'm closer."*

A Change is Coming

He Conveyed the Blessing

He led them to Bethany. He says, *"This is where I'm going to impart and then depart."* It was Jesus saying, *"I've carried the burden."* Not only did He carry the burden, but He conveyed the blessing. Look at what it says in Luke Chapter 24:50b, *"...and he lifted up his hands, and blessed them."* Now, to lift up the hands and bless them, that is the Old Testament because only the high priest could speak the blessing over the people. He lifted His hands because it was signifying that the blessing was coming, not from the priest, it was coming down from glory through the priest to the people of God. He says, *"I am speaking a blessing over the people."* The priest would come and he would have blood spattered garments on. He had a white robe on, and it was blood spattered because he had been in making the sin offering and the burnt offering and he was in the guilt offering. He had been giving the offerings and he was covered in blood. So, he's covered in blood. He would take off his bloody robe and put on his glory robe.

See, Jesus took off the bloody robe and put on His glory robe. That's why He could walk through doors and they were still locked. And I don't know, but we serve a risen Savior that has glory upon Him. You see, because Jesus said, *"I have to fulfill the law."* Leviticus 9:22 tells us about the Aaronic priesthood, and Aaron would come down from making the offering and he would speak a blessing. Aaron lifted his hands toward the people and blessed them coming down from offering the sin offering, the burnt offering, and the peace offerings, and he would speak the blessing over the people. Do you know what that blessing is? It's in Numbers 6:24-26: *"The Lord bless thee, and keep thee: The Lord make his face to shine upon thee, and be gracious unto thee: The Lord lift up his countenance upon thee, and give thee peace."* What is that? He is saying, *"I'm speaking of the blessing that, if I've got the countenance of the Lord and the light of the Lord shining upon me, then my life is blessed."*

I'm so glad He lifted His countenance. What does that mean? Let me just break that down a little bit. To lift His countenance literally means that God bowed down to my level. That means He bowed down and He came down. He got small. Why? Because He said, *"I've got to meet My children right where they are."* That's why He said, *"We serve not a high priest who cannot be touched with the feelings of our infirmities but was on all points touched and tempted even as we are tempted yet without sin."* So, blessed be the name of our God that He bowed down to our level and put His countenance on us.

So, I thank God for His words, but there's something to be said about these hands. Look, you're going to catch these hands. What? He lifted up His hands and He blessed them. Yes, that thing just shook me because whenever you saw Jesus using His hands, somebody walked away changed. The leper came to Him and bowed down in Matthew 8:2 and said, *"If thou wilt, thou can make me clean."* Jesus said, *"I will."* Then He reached out and touched him, and the man was clean. He left better than he came in Jesus' name. Peter's mother-in-law was sick with a fever and the Bible says that Jesus came in the room, stood over her, and touched her hand, and the fever had to leave her. Has anyone ever had Jesus touch you? Oh, He touched me and I've never been the same. He touched me and He delivered me. He touched me and He set me free.

One evening, all kinds of sick people and demon-possessed people were brought to Jesus and the Bible says, they laid them at His feet. He spoke a word and drove out demons, but He laid hands and maimed folks were made whole. What is maimed? Maimed means you're missing a limb. He laid His hands and limbs that were not there, appeared. I'm talking about a move of God. I'm talking about something that was impossible. I don't know about you, but I'd love to see a move, where others would say that's impossible. But that's how God is moving. Yes, He touched them and they were better.

One day, there was a multitude of people who were hungry. They took the lad's lunch and put it in the hands of Jesus. He blessed it. He broke it and the multitudes were fed.

A man by the name of Jairus had a daughter who was at the point of death. By the time they got to Jesus, she had died. Jesus put them out of the house and said, *"Talitha cumi."* He grabbed her by the hand and the Bible says, she got up. It's about His hands. His hands heal. His hands deliver. His hands set free. His hands make us whole. I want you to say, *"Lay Your hands on me, Jesus."*

When I see His hands, the nail-scarred hands, I won't have to wonder who Jesus is because He still bears the marks in His body of the price that was paid for my sin and yours. Your sin has been forgiven. He paid the price for them.

He Contemplated that Break

I want you to see something that the Lord showed me in Luke 24:50-51, it says, *"...and he lifted up his hands, and blessed them. And it came to pass, while he blessed them, he was parted from them, and carried up into heaven."* I want us to contemplate the break. What is the break? Let's look at this, while Jesus is blessing and being a blessing, He's parted from them. It was an interruption in the midst of the blessing. Something happens that parted them from Jesus. There was no warning. Jesus is in mid-sentence; He's interrupted by this parting from them.

I just want you to think of how the people that you've had in your life that have gone on to be with the Lord, how one day they were blessing you and it seems right in the midst of them blessing you, they are parted from you. Well, it might have been your mother, might have been your father, might have been your uncle, might have been your auntie, but they were parted from us because the Lord sent something for them.

There's a break right while Jesus is being a blessing. I'm enjoying the presence. I'm enjoying the blessings. Then all of a sudden, there's a parting. What is it reminding us of? It's reminding us that you've got to make the most of every moment in this life because we never know when while in the midst of blessing, there'll be a parting. Be ye also ready for we know not the day nor the hour when the Son of Man shall appear. There was a parting in the midst of a blessing.

The word *parting* means to be set apart. But it's not a permanent separation. It's a temporary separation, and I don't know who's still grieving the loss of their loved one. The Lord told me to tell you, *"They're just dearly departed."* This means it's only for a temporary season. You will see them again. It's not goodbye. It's simply, see you later.

I know they sing the song, "It's so hard to say goodbye to yesterday," but Glory be to God for tomorrow. There was a parting that somebody we loved had to be taken away from us. How have you dealt with your interruptions? Your brother is gone. How have you dealt with the loss of a son? Still angry with God? Are you still saying you shouldn't have taken him too soon? Are you saying blessed be it's only temporary? Farewell my brother. Farewell my son. Farewell my daughter. Farewell my wife. Farewell my husband. You've got to say it's only temporary. This too shall pass. Farewell. We shall meet again in the sweet by and by. Yes, it was a temporary parting.

A Change is Coming

The second part of Luke 24:51 says, *"...he was parted from them, and carried up."* Carried up. Why did God need Jesus? Jesus could have just gone; from here to there. But He was carried. Much like Elijah when he jumped on the fiery chariot and got out of here. It says He was parted. I wonder, did the same kind of chariot come for Jesus. But what is God saying?

There's something deeper here. What is God saying that Jesus has to be seen leaving? Who did we say the scripture said was the prince of the power of the air? Satan. Thinking he got things on lockdown while saying, *"I wish somebody would try to come up through these airways without my permission. I wish he would try it."* Jesus didn't ascend. He said, *"I am not going to just disappear and appear in glory. No! I'm walking through the prince of the power of the air. Through his territory and letting him know I'm the big dog up in here."*

You've got to know that Satan's power is not equal to the power of God. He's a subordinate. He is not an equal. You give him too much credit. He's a defeated foe. He's a liar and the father of lies. I can bless the Lord even in an interruption. He said, *"Even though I'm leaving, I'm not leaving forever."* Ten days later, they got the Holy Ghost.

He says, *"I'm trying to let you know that the prince has no more dominion. His power has been broken, and I came so that those who have been oppressed of the devil shall be set free."*

Thessalonians 4:16-17 says, *"For the Lord himself shall descend from heaven with a shout, with the voice of the archangel, and with the trump of God: and the dead in Christ shall rise first: Then we which are alive and remain shall be caught up together with them in the clouds, to meet the Lord in the air: and so shall we ever be with the Lord."* What is the Lord saying? There's going to come a time when we are going to be parted and carried. I want you to know that the glory that's coming down will be on the earth is not where we will be when we die. He said, *"To be absent in the body is to be present with the Lord."* So, that means we are in a place called paradise. Remember what Jesus said on the cross? He said, *"Today you will be with me in paradise."* We don't stay in a grave, not for those that believe. He already kicked the back door out of the grave and now I'm resting with Him. I'm in Abraham's bosom. You've got to believe what the Bible says, not just what you heard is in the Bible. You have to know it and hear it for yourself.

Celebrated the Bounty

Last but not least, they celebrate the bounty. Listen to this, we are continuing in Luke 24:51-52, *"And it came to pass while he blessed them he was parted from them and carried up into heaven, and they worshiped him..."* He was gone, but they worshiped Him.

Now, we are dealing with people who are well-versed in Old Testament theology. These are not novices. These are those who were raised up in the scriptures. Exodus 20:3 says, *"You shall have no other gods before me."* So, you could not bow down to anything or anyone who was not God. But they fell down and they worshiped Him. Why? Because a change has happened. They realized that they were not focused on what somebody else said in the Old Testament because they experienced their own encounter with God in the times that they were living. So, they fell down and they worshipped Jesus. This reveals a level of revelation that nobody had ever had before. Jesus never stopped anybody that worshiped Him. The angels said not to worship them, but Jesus was different. Jesus knew that He was God in the flesh and yes, your worship is received. You've got to declare your worship is for real.

A Change is Coming

Why would they worship Jesus?

The first reason was because of what they had seen. When Jesus walks to them on the water in the fourth watch of the night, that's 2 a.m. to 6 a.m. The wind whipped waves, there was a storm raging, and Jesus is not even wet. They were amazed at the fact He was walking on the water. Why? Because He has dominion even over gravity. He said, *"Even the laws that are in this world; I'm not subject to them. I supersede them. I'm the one who put them in place."* So, every law bows to Him. Sickness bows to Him.

We see in Matthew 14:33 where it says, *"Then they that were in the ship came and worshipped him, saying, Of a truth thou art the Son of God."* The Lord told me to tell you, *"When I bring you out of a storm, you better give me some worship."* Matthew 28:17 says, *"And when they saw him, they worshipped him: but some doubted."* This was after Jesus' resurrection and He was on the Mount of Galilee in Galilee, and they fell down when they saw Him after the resurrection. They saw Him and fell down and worshiped Him, but some doubted; they were in His presence and still wondering. I just wonder how many of us have ever sat in a worship service while all that praise and worship was going on and you just sat there doubting and saying, *"It doesn't take all of that."* Why is it that you don't say that when your team is winning the game? You see the game is going to be over, but God is still on the throne.

They were struggling with the revelation, but they fell down and worshiped Him. Because of His presence, they worshiped Him; because of His proclamation and His word, they worshiped Him; because of His provision, they worshiped Him; because of His power, they worshipped Him. They went to Jerusalem with great joy.

Now, if you remember when Jesus said, *"I must go to Jerusalem."* He knew that He was going there to be persecuted and to die. He said, "Come on, we got to go." One of the disciples said, *"Well, let us go and die with Him."*

Some of us don't want to go over there because we know what's getting ready to happen. All of a sudden, they've been empowered because of who's presence they've been in. I'm trying to get somebody to declare, *"I've got a brand-new courage today."* What is fear but courage that has said its prayers.

They worshiped Him and were continually in the temple. Jesus went to the temple every Sabbath but it says, *"They were continually in the temple."* We come once a week but they were going to stay there continually. Their actions were saying, *"We're going to bump the traditions but we going to get in here and learn about our Savior."* We come continually, which means that they never stopped coming.

There are many today that it doesn't take but a little bit to keep them from coming on a Sunday morning. Let's not even begin to discuss a weeknight service. Some of you looked out the window on Sunday morning and said, *"It's cloudy, I don't know if I'm going."* Every preacher across this land hates when they roll over in the morning and hear a little thunder. *"Oh Jesus, they aren't coming this morning. They go to work when it's raining, but they fail to come to the House of the Lord to worship You."*

It said that they were continually, but there isn't any more sacrifice; nobody is sacrificing any more. Why? Because we say we got our lamb. We don't need to get a turtle dove. We don't need to get an ox. We don't need to get an ass. We've already got our lamb without a blemish. His name is Jesus. Jesus went every Sabbath, but He said, *"We continue in the temple praising and blessing God."* But there was a sacrifice. Hebrews 13:15 says it this way, *"By him therefore let us offer the sacrifice of praise to God continually, that is, the fruit of*

A Change is Coming

our lips giving thanks to his name." He said, *"I'm going to offer the sacrifice of praise unto God continually giving Him the fruit of my lips and giving thanks unto the Lord. It's all about Him."*

In John 1:3-4 says it this way, *"All things were made by him; and without him was not anything made that was made. In him was life; and the life was the light of men."* It's in Him. John 3:16 says it this way, *"For God so loved the world, that he gave his only begotten Son, that whosoever believeth in him shall not should not perish, but have everlasting life."* John 4:24 said it this way, *"God is a Spirit: and they that worship him must worship him in spirit and in truth."* Acts 17:28 says it this way, *"For in him we live, and move, and have our being..."* It's in Him. II Corinthians 1:20 says it this way, *"For all the promises of God in him are yea, and in him Amen, unto the glory of God by us."* Glory to God. Philippians 2:9-11 says, *"Wherefore God also hath highly exalted him, and given him a name which is above every name: That at the name of Jesus every knee should bow, of things in heaven, and things in the earth, and things under the earth; And every tongue should confess that Jesus Christ is Lord, to the glory of God the Father."*

It's in Him. It's Him who woke me up this morning, it's Him who started me on my way and made a way out of no way. It's Him who's keeping me in my body and my mind. It's Him who's watching over my children and grandchildren. It's Him who's watching over my house. It's Him who's watching over the church and the country. It's Him who soothes my sorrow. It's Him who gives me hope for tomorrow. It's Him who is the way out of no way. It's Him who is water in dry places. When others walk away, it's Him. When others falter, it's Him. When others talk about you, it's Him. You've got to say, I don't care what you say about me. The more you talk about me, the more I'll bend my knees. Talk about me as much as you please. It's Him It's Him who turned that thing around. It's Him. I promise you that if you need Him right now, it's Him. Turn it around, Lord. Deliver, Lord. It's Him. Set free, Lord. It's Him. A change has come. It's Him. A change, glory to God, has come. It's Him, Jesus. Thank you, Jesus. When I couldn't see my way, it was Him. Thank you, Jesus. When I couldn't talk to anyone else, it was Him.

Father, in the name of Jesus, we thank you for your Son. We thank you that the change has come. Amen!

Chapter 4
Footwork

John 13:14-15

When we look at the book of St. John, we see work from the onset:

- John 1: The Bible says the word became flesh and dwelled among us. That was work.
  John 2: The Bible says the Word was working and turning water into wine.
- John 3: The Word continues the work and tells Nicodemus he must be born again.
  John 4: The Word keeps on working and tells a woman at a well that God is a spirit, and they that worship Him must worship Him in Spirit and in truth.
- John 5: The Word spies on a man who laid at a pool for 38 years and begins to work and tell that man rise, take up his bed, and walk.

- John 6: The Word is still working, for it takes two fish and five loaves of bread and feeds the multitudes.
- John 7: The Word is still working, and it says, *"I am the fountain if any man thirsts, let him come to me and drink."*
- John 8: The Word is working as a great defender for the woman who was caught in the act of adultery. He says, *"Where are those that condemn you?"* She said, *"No man, Lord."* He said, *"Neither do I condemn me go and sin no more."*
- John 9: They happen upon a man who was blind from his mother's womb and the Word begins to work. They say who sinned this man or his parents that he was born blind. Jesus said, *"Neither this man nor his parents have sinned, but this was done that the glory of God might be revealed in his life."*
- John 10: The Word is still working because it becomes the Good Shepherd.
  John 11: He's working because He said, *"I am the resurrection and the life."*
- John 12: He said, *"If I be lifted up above the earth, I'll draw all men unto me."*
  John 13: He's a servant and He said, *"I have washed your feet therefore you ought to wash one another's feet."*

The Setting

Let me give you the setting. This is my first point, the setting. I want you to come down to Jerusalem with me, come down to the dusty streets of Jerusalem, come as the disciples are leaving home. Think with me for a minute as

Foot Work

your boo is saying, "*I'll be back in a minute.*" You have got some questions for him, "*Where are you going? Who are you going to be with? Who is going to be over there?*" His response may be, "*I'm headed to have dinner with the Master.*" In return, she says, "*Uh-huh. Is that her name? Where are you going? Whose house? I need to know.*"

Just walk with me for a minute. They are getting themselves together, and they leave their homes going to the place that Jesus has appointed for them to meet and have supper with Him. He said, "*Go to a place that is prepared so that we might have the Passover meal.*"

So, walk with them as the sun is setting and they feel the heat of the sand between their toes that was heated by the sun of the day. It is now dark, and there's a breeze blowing in from the desert. The moon is shining, and you can see the shadows that are long and cast along the ground. They're headed to suffer with Jesus. As they approach the place that He's appointed for them, they see the staircase and the light on in the room. They know the Master has gone before them. They ascend the staircase, and they're wondering what shall await them. They can even smell the roasted lamb in the air because the lamb is what they must have for the Passover meal.

In Exodus 12, they talk about the Passover, and you had to have a lamb that was prepared with bitter herbs, so they can smell it. There's barbecue going on all over the city. Everybody is in preparation for the Passover meal. There's a wonderful smell in the air. They have conversations between one another about the happening of the day, and once they get to the room, the door opens into a great banquet hall. The lights are low, and there in the center of room, seated at the table is Jesus.

They bring their burdens. They bring their bruises. They bring their baggage into the room with Jesus, and just like us, we have all descended upon this place in the presence of our Savior and we've all got some baggage. We've all got some bruises. We've all got some burdens but blessed be the name of our God, He is the burden lifter. He is Jehovah Rapha, the God that heals thee. He is a heavy load sharer. I just want you to know that we serve a risen Savior.

He was waiting for them and when they came into the room, they did not look for anything but Him. I came looking for Him because I've got a burden that only He can lift. I came looking for Him because I've got a bruise that only He can heal. I came looking for Him because I've got baggage that only He can unpack. I need the presence of my Savior.

So, they press into the room and they're sitting there, and they look and there is a table. This is not a table like you see in our homes that is waist high, and you pull your chair up under it. No, it's rather low and you have to get low to get to sit at this table. Some of us can't get to the table of God because it's too low for us to get there. We're not humble. We're too prideful. We think it's beneath us to come to the table with Jesus, but He said, *"In order to get to this table, you must get low."*

How low can you go to get to the table of the Lord Jesus? In order to sit at this table, you've got to get lower than your academic accomplishments and that diploma on the wall; they won't help you. You've got to get lower than your bank account; it is of no assistance to you. You've got to get lower than your exclusive neighborhood; it is not even a factor in this matter. You've got to get lower than your nice car and your fine clothes and your smell goods; they serve no relevance. You've got to get low if you want to get to the table with Jesus.

Foot Work

So, they had to come in and get low. We need to say, *"Lord I've got to get low because I want You to lift me high. I want to lift You first because I'm going to lift You, and I can't be lifted without You. So, I'm coming lower because as I come low, You will lift me up."* Humble yourself under the mighty hand of God and He'll exalt you in due season. I'm lifted because I'm with Jesus.

They come to the table. All of us have a table in our lives. You are sitting at my table right now. And guess what? I'm at your table. We are at one another's table, and you know who you've got at your table. Some folks we wish would never get up, but there's some folks we wish would have never sat down. I'm still trying to get them away from my table. The table represents a place of communion and a place of revelation. It's a place of impartation; it is an opportunity to exercise influence. It's a place to make decisions and effect change. So, if I come to the place of the table with Jesus, then He gives me an opportunity to exact an exchange for a change in my life when I come to the table.

Did you see the shift? You thought I was talking about making a change for something else. No, the change begins with us. If I'm going to be at the table with Jesus, He said, *"You do not have any room to negotiate this thing. You either give it or you can keep it. I'm not going to force your hand. You've got a burden; lay it down. I'm tired of you saying you gave it to me, but then you pick it up when you walk away."* I dare you to leave it right there and watch what God will do with it.

I'm seated at the table because there's some biblical record of those who came to a table. If you don't remember, Moses was called to the table with Pharaoh and he said, *"Let my people go."* There was no negotiation. You're going to either do it or you're not, and there is going to be some consequences if you don't.

Esther was called to the table with King Ahasuerus and when she went to the table, she said, *"This wicked Haman is the one."* Haman had some plans for the people of God, but the plans that he made for them were the plans that hung him. I wish somebody knew something about others digging a ditch for you and they fall in. You don't have to worry about it; let the Lord handle it.

Not only were Moses and Esther called to the table, but what about Mephibosheth, the one who believed he was nothing better than a dead dog? The one who believed he was down in Lo-debar, a place of no communication. The one who was a king's kid who is now in a place that he never imagined he would be. Here comes David and he sent for Mephibosheth. There're some Mephibosheth's here, those who have been dropped by time, dropped by circumstance, dropped by situation, dropped by those who thought they would be there for you forever and they walked away from you. But the Lord said, *"When others drop you, I will pick you up because I am God, the Alpha and Omega, the beginning and the ending."*

Jesus called them to the table. Now just walk with me for a minute. I'm painting a picture here. I want you to see how He called them to the table to sit with Him. Notice that they brought their dirt with them. Do you mean to tell me I'm walking with Jesus, but I still got dirty feet? How could my feet get dirty while I'm walking with Jesus? While I'm lifting my hands, while I'm saying amen, while I've got my dance, and while tears are streaming down my face, I can still have dirty feet. I'm preaching the gospel and still have a little bit of dirt on my feet. He said, *"You can have a wrong thought and you've already sinned."* You've got to be careful so that you don't get caught

Foot Work

thinking you aren't dirty and possibly may even stink. Some of us don't believe our feet stink.

You go about your business thinking you were all right, thinking you're not as bad as others, but in reality, you are worse. They're at the table with dirty feet, communing and praising with dirty feet. It is cute you got your steps together, but dirty feet. Lord, help us with our dirty feet.

You need to put in some footwork. They were in varying degrees of separation at the table because it was not a round table, it was a rectangular table. So, watch now you've got everybody seated at the table. You know that the disciples did not look like Europeans and that picture that Michelangelo painted that he was not there. You do understand that if you went to Asia, the people who have pictures in Asia of Jesus, the eyes are slanted because it's a representation of them because He was made in our likeness and in our image. So then if you go to Africa, He's got a wide nose and full lips and woolly hair. Why? Because He's made in our image and in our likeness and He says, *"He can identify with us."* So, if you go to Europe. Guess what? He may be represented with long hair and blue eyes. Nobody walked the streets of Jerusalem in that sun that long and be that fair skin. Jesus is a representation of us all; nobody corners the market on Jesus.

Now His glorified state sounds more like that of the African decent with hair like wool, feet like burnish brass and He'd been burned in the fire. We were all at the table. At that table, there were differing degrees of separation between them.

Jesus is at the table, and I wonder, where Jesus was really sitting. He is the head of the church. If I'm at the head of my house, guess where my wife puts my plate, at the head of the table, and then guess what? She sits at the other end of the table, right? Not that she's opposing me, but she is balancing me. Just walk with my sanctified imagination and as I was studying, I just sat down, and I started to think about, where was Jesus? I'm sure He was at the head of the table. Even if He chose to sit on either side of the table, it would be like this; here I am Jesus, then there would be somebody who wanted to be on the opposite side of Jesus. What am I saying? Some of us are in opposition to Jesus. We have differing opinions about what our lives ought to be consistent with. When you play cards, you're playing against them. You're sitting in opposition because you're against me and I'm against you. Jesus on one side of the table, disciples on the other. I could imagine it was Judas who said, *"This is my seat because I'm in opposition to Jesus."*

Then there was one of the disciples was close to Jesus that but he had to lay on His breast. He wanted to hear the very heartbeat of Jesus. I just wonder if you are one that says, *"I've got to lean on His breast. I've got to lean on His breast when my heart is broken. I've got to lean on His breast when I don't know which way to turn. I've got to lean on His breast when I don't know what to do next. I'll lean on His breast until He speaks to me. I'll lean on His breast until the way is made. I've got to hear it."*

They're across the table with opposition, wanting things their way. Some of us know folks in our families that sit on the opposite side of the table from us. They're the opposite of us politically. They're the opposite of us socially. They're the opposite of us relationally. They're the opposite of us religiously. There are so many opposites that we encounter in this life, but Jesus, comes to give us an even playing field. I don't know about you, but wherever He is, that's where I want to be.

Foot Work

So, I just wonder if somebody might have come up and said, *"This is my seat Jesus. I'm the head."* Then everybody else said, *"Man, you need to get out of the way. that's Jesus' spot; move, you need to move."* Don't act like we don't get prideful. I'm sure there have been times in your life when you made the decision to take up the position of Jesus in your own life. Have you said things like, *"I'm grown. I do what I want to do."*

You want the end of the table? Quit trying to be the head even over Jesus. Submit yourself to Jesus. But when they got to the table, everybody ate. Everybody had the roast lamb, bitter herbs, the unleavened bread, and everybody partook in the meal. It was wonderful and I do not know about you, but I didn't go to church, not to eat. They came to eat even with dirty feet.

Where is Jesus at your table? I may not be dotting every "I" and crossing every "T," but I'm going to eat. I've got some faults, some failures, and some fractures, but I'm going to eat. I stumbled and I've fallen, but I didn't stay down, so I'm going to eat. What about you? Are you going to eat? I don't care what you say. I don't care what you are doing beside me; I came to eat today.

The Saints

When they came, none of them thought about dirty feet. It was customary to wash feet. Nobody even said to Jesus, *"Jesus, You had to walk here. Can I wash your feet for you?"* Jesus had already prepared the place when they got there, they couldn't even do the simple things. Why is it that so many of us once we come up, we forget the simple things?

You used to be humble, now your haughty. You don't wash feet anymore. You don't serve anybody; everybody has to serve you now. You are beyond that; I don't have time for that. You have an attitude that says, *"Do you see the house we live in, the neighborhood we live in and the neighbors we have?"* All while having a haughty and holier-than-thou attitude and a belief of moral superiority, but let me shed some light on your situation; everything you have is because He prepared it. Nothing you have achieved has been on your own, He has made it available to you and for you. Take the time to acknowledge Him as the Lord of your life.

He told the saints to wash one another's feet. Think about it; you can't get somebody else's feet until Jesus washes your feet. Why do you talk about the speck in your brother's eye, the speck in your sister's eye, and you got a plank in your eye? You know, it's a shame that she got that daughter down there who isn't married and have five kids. You're out there gossiping about somebody's business. You've got a plank.

Now think about it. He said, *"Wash one another's feet."* But not all dirt is seen; we've got some dirt on the bacterial level. That's the one that creates the smell, that bacteria that's between the toes. Not all of us want to get between those toes.

Why did they need foot washing? Because back then, there weren't any sidewalks. They had to walk the path that the wagons went through. You do know they had some donkeys and some sheep. Sheep and donkeys drop stuff in the street and if you are not careful, you are going to step in it. Some of us have stepped in some stuff and got it on our sandals up between our toes, and now you want me to wash your feet? Here I am. I have got to deal with your mess. God said, *"Because we are in the same body we must get involved in one another's lives."* That doesn't mean you're nosey. That doesn't mean you gossip about it. It means that you express enough love towards another

Foot Work

brother or another sister that will help them get their feet cleaned up.

I know you think your feet are clean. Can I tell you something though? When you are preparing the water for your brothers and your sisters, don't make it too hot. See, refining with the fire is God's work. We are to relieve, refresh, and restore our brothers and sisters, not scald them. Take your time to get the water just right for them so that when they put their feet in it, it's soothing. You don't come to me so I can beat you over your head about your dirty feet. We already know they are dirty; that is why we are washing them. Guess what? I got my feet in water, too. I don't have anything to say about your toes being turned that way, because my toes turned the other way. But the standard is Jesus and Jesus has clean feet.

How do we do the work?

Number one, do the work carefully. You don't grab and jerk on anybody's feet. Speak gently; don't say, "*Look, give me these nasty feet.*" You know how some folks are just grabbing your foot. Don't grab my foot like that; be gentle.

Number two, do this work cheerfully. Act like you are glad to be doing what you are doing. Don't be that McDonald's employee, "*What do you want?*" You start by saying, "*I think I want...*" Then they rush you by saying, "*You've been standing in line for five minutes and you don't know what you want.*" Do it cheerfully. Why? Because the joy of the Lord is your strength, and that joy should show up in your service.

As a pastor, I always encourage the choir because when you're singing, everybody sees your face. If you don't look happy about it, nobody else is going to be happy about it. Do the work cheerfully. Many don't want low jobs, but some of these jobs are necessary jobs that you need to do with a cheerful attitude and not begrudgingly.

Number three, do the work thoroughly. When the boys were younger, one of their responsibilities was to cut the grass. I would instruct them how I liked it to look and expected that it would be done as instructed. I would remind them, *"Now, when you turn, don't miss that grass when you turn. Put that wheel back on the other side and then push on down."* They would say, *"Daddy, you always tell us, you missed the spot."* We have to do the work and do it thoroughly the first time, then you won't have to go back out and do it again. I remember one day, I come home after being gone all day, and I looked at the yard and shook my head. I went right in the house calling for the boys to tell them, *"You missed a bunch of spots."* They would respond saying, *"But Daddy, I took a shower."* Many may think I was being hard on them, but these are young men being trained for their future, so get out there and do it, right. I wanted them to learn, so I told them, *"I don't care. If you hadn't missed those spots, we wouldn't be talking right now. So, go back out there and get the yard right, just like I like it."*

Number four, the Savior. Jesus reveals some things to us in this transaction. By washing feet, He is saying forgiving is mandatory. He said if you don't forgive your Heavenly Father, He will not forgive your trespasses. He was washing the feet and feeding the very person who was going to betray Him. He was washing the feet and feeding the very person who is going to deny Him three times. He was washing the feet and feeding the very person who's going to doubt Him. But guess what? He could not ascend to His rightful place without being betrayed and without being denied. I know it's not popular, but it is the truth. Some folks are a part of your assignment. You had to be

Foot Work

hurt. Jesus knew what they were trying to do, still feeding them and giving them drink. If your enemy hungers, feed them or if they thirst, give them drink, but not poison them.

Forgiving is mandatory. Reconciliation is optional. Some people just do not like you. You can do all you can for them, and they are still working against you. Jesus said, *"Whatever you going to do, do it quickly."* He knew the heart of Judas. He knew Peter was going to deny Him and that Thomas was going to doubt Him, and still, He did not say, *"Get out of here."* Judas was stealing money. Jesus didn't say, *"Boy I know you're a thief."* He washed his feet.

What do you do with people who you know are crooked? Some of us wouldn't spit on them to put them out if they were on fire. But you're the Christian. The Bible says, *"Don't render evil for evil but overcome evil with good."* We tend to forget about that scripture and try to justify our actions by saying, *"They did me dirty. I can't wait to get even."*

We're passive-aggressive. Wives get passive-aggressive with the husband. Because you're mad, you decide, *"I'll fix a plate for everybody but him."* You must understand your relationship is an extension of your worship. How you treat your wife is an extension of your worship. How you treat your husband, if you don't have one yet, you practice. I'm clearing out a space for my boo.

He said that reconciliation is optional. I'm here, but that doesn't always mean we're going to be reconciled. We just have to make sure our heart is right.

What's your heart posture? You've still got some malice against your baby mama. Still got some malice against your "used to be?" Still upset about the way they treated you and you can't hear their name without gritting your teeth. You are not delivered. You're talking about everything's alright, but everything is not alright. If we start talking about it, I see your cheeks jumping. You are gritting your teeth and trying to smile at the same time. The devil is a lie. If you can't stand the sound of his voice on the other end of the phone when he calls about the kids, you are not delivered. You've got to ask the Lord, *"Help me with my heart and wash my feet because they are nasty."*

He says, *"Not only is forgiving mandatory and reconciliation is optional, but revelation is required."* God will allow hurt to reveal your heart. You didn't know who he was until he hurt you. You didn't know who she was until she hurt you. You went in prayer and said, *"Oh God, why did you let it happen? And why didn't you tell me who he was?"* However, all along, you didn't hear your sister saying, *"He's no good."* When your mama said, *"Girl get away from that boy,"* that wasn't your mama; that was Me.

So, He says, *"I'm trying to get you to a place. I got to hurt you to reveal the heart."* When you got the COVID-19 shot and it really didn't hurt, you went on about your business and felt a little pain later from the injections. Then some of us still came down with COVID. My wife and I came down with the disease, and it lasted about 18 hours, and we were back in the kitchen, eating. He said, *"You took the shot. You might get sick, but you won't die."*

When we come into circumstances, we may take a shot. He said, *"But because I'm with you, you won't die. Greater is He that is in me than He that is in the world."* I've taken some shots, but I am not dead. I'm still standing and glorifying the name of our God and our Savior. I lift Him on high because it was Him. I feel pain today, but I won't die tomorrow.

Foot Work

I just started seeing the word keep on working because after we leave chapter 13 and step into chapter 14, we hear the Word saying, *"Let not your hearts be troubled: ye believe in God, believe also in me. In my Father's house are many mansions: if it were not so, I would have told you. I go to prepare a place for you."* Jesus was giving us a glimpse in chapter 13 when He went and prepared the upper room. He said, *"Do you know you're going to the upper room?"* I'm getting ready for the upper room. I'm getting ready to go to another place. I'm getting higher than I've ever been before because He's already gone before me and prepared the way. Then I turned over to John 15 and the Bible says, *"I am the vine, my Father is the husbandman."* He said, *"If ye abide in Me, and My words abide in you, ye shall ask what ye will, and it shall be done unto you."*

- John 16: The Word is still working. He said, *"I want you to get ready because I'm sending another Comforter."*
- John 17: Jesus is working in the garden and praying for us. He said, *"Father send the glory; that I had before I came here. I've glorified it once and I'll glorify it again."* I want Him to glorify it again. Send your glory, God.
- John 18: They came to the garden, and they were seeking Jesus. He said, *"Whom do thou seek?"* They said, *"Jesus of Nazareth."* He said, *"I am,"* and the word was so strong they couldn't even stand. The Bible said, *"They fell back."* They got up and came again. He said, *"Who are you seeking?"* They said, *"Jesus of Nazareth."* He said, *"I told you I am,"* and they fell back again.
- John 19: They scourged Him, they whipped Him on the whipping post 39 lashes, but He couldn't die there, He kept on serving. They nailed Him

to an old rugged cross, and He said, "*Father, forgive them for they know not what they do.*" What was He doing? He was still working. They hung Him high; they stretched Him wide, but He didn't stop working. He said, "*Today you're going to be with me in paradise.*" I'm ready to go to a new place in Jesus. I'm going to wash my feet until He comes back for me. He hung His head and then He died.

- John 20: He rose on the third day morning. He said, "*I've got all power in Heaven and in Earth in my hands.*"
- John 21: Jesus asks Peter; "*Peter, do you love me?*" Peter said, "*I love you.*" Jesus said, "*Peter, do you love me?*" He said, "*Yes I love you.*" He said, "Peter, "*Do you love me?*" And it said Peter was grieved. Wait a minute, "*You deny me three times and I can't ask you three times?*" That's us. He said, "*Yes Lord, you know I love you.*" He said, "*Feed my lambs, feed my sheep, and feed my people.*"

In Acts 2, Peter preached, and 3,000 souls were added to the church. What a wonderful Savior to be able to wash the dirt from Peter's feet and then use him for His glory.

Chapter 5
How to Defeat Discouragement

1 Corinthians 15:57-58

Discouragement is a dissatisfaction with the past. It is a distaste for the present. It is a distrust of the future. It is an ingratitude for the blessings of yesterday. It is an indifference to the opportunities that are presented today. It is an insecurity regarding strength for tomorrow. It is an unawareness of the presence of beauty. It is uncaring for the needs of others. It is an unbelief of the promises of old. It is simply an impatience with time. It's immaturity of thought and it is impoliteness with God. Such is discouragement. It is a loss of confidence or enthusiasm. It is disheartening. It is to be without courage to do, and there are at least three things that bring us to that place of discouragement.

Friction

Number one, it is friction. There's a strain in the relationship and you are facing a crossroads, and you don't know what to do. Friction happens when two connected things are moving in two opposite directions. So, I wonder if somebody is already experiencing discouragement because you are experiencing friction. You and those you are connected to are going in two different directions and because of it, there is a level of discouragement that you are dealing with right now and you came with much on your plate and you're wondering, *"Is there a word from the Lord?"* The Lord says, *"You can deal with the discouragement in spite of the friction."*

Fatigue

Not only is there the friction, but the other thing that creates discouragement is fatigue. Americans are the most exhausted people in the world, and 30 to 50 percent of Americans suffer from some kind of sleep deprivation. A tossing and turning all night long simply because you've got some discouragement in your heart and in your mind. You're wondering, *"Lord, am I ever going to get over this? Can I get out of this? Which way do I turn right now, God?"* But the Lord told me to tell you, *"Be still and know that I am God."*

Many sleep, but they never rest. Do you know that billions of dollars are made on sleep aids? Things that people take so that they can go to sleep. Do you know what was going on with Michael Jackson? He had everything but couldn't get a good night's rest. I just wondered not only with Michael Jackson, but Prince, too. They had all that you could ever imagine of anybody, all the talent, all the creativity, but they could not rest. I just wonder if it's the lack of a relationship with a sovereign God who pushes us to a place where we have no place to rest. David said, *"When I was in distress, I lay down and rested and the Lord sustained me"* (Psalm 3:5). So, I get rest not because I take a sleep aid. I get rest because the sovereign Lord watches over me. So, there is no need for me to stay up all night long because He never sleeps, nor does He slumber. He's always watching over me; all day, all night, angels watching over me.

Feelings of Failure

So, it's not just friction and fatigue. The last thing that aids in discouragement is feelings of failure. This happens to us all, especially for those that are in ministry because you feel like you give everything, and things still don't go the way you want them to go. If you're not in ministry, then it can be in your marriage. You say, *"I'm giving everything, and it still doesn't seem to be going."* Notice this point is not failure, but the feelings of failure. Feelings can and will mislead you. They'll lead you down the wrong path. That's why the Apostle Paul said, *"Walk by faith..."* (2 Corinthians 5:7). He didn't say walk by feelings. You've got to say, *"Lord help me, even in my unbelief. I don't want to just be led because I'm feeling a certain way. I've got to be led by my faith."*

Do you know that you don't feel your way into doing anything? If you wake up in the morning and it's time for you to go to work, you don't feel it, but you get up and go anyway. There may be some days you're with your honey and you're not feeling it, but you love them anyway because God has called you to this place and this time and this season in your life and you've got to walk through a thing even if you're not feeling it. Sometimes your children might get on your nerves, but it isn't about how you feel.

The reason I'm talking about discouragement is because Paul is writing to a church filled with people who are discouraged.

He's writing to people who are weary and worn out. He's writing to people that are on the brink of giving up. I just want to ask if I can poll you. Have you ever felt like giving up? Have you ever felt like throwing in the towel? Have you ever felt like saying to heck with this? But the Lord was saying, *"No, it's time to press in even the more. I want you to keep walking in this because this difficulty is going to strengthen you. This difficulty is going to solidify you. It's going to stabilize you after you have suffered a little while."* Let's look at 1 Peter 5:10, it says, *"But the God of all grace, who hath called us unto his eternal glory by Christ Jesus, after that ye have suffered a while, make you perfect, stablish, strengthen, settle you."* Then He shall establish me, then He shall settle me down.

Some of us need to be settled. You can't be a loose cannon; you need to settle down. My mother used to say, *"Get somewhere and settle down."* On a rainy day, my grandmother would turn the TV off, take the phone off the hook, and say, *"Now shut up!"* We had to sit in the dark and she'd tell us, *"You better not say nothing about it's hot in here. Just shut up, the Lord is working."*

They are praying for rest and rest didn't come. They're looking for a blessing and all they get is a stressing. Have you ever been in a place where you wondered where God was? I know with our cute little church sayings; we like to make people believe that we know where God is at all times. But if people that wrote the Bible looked for God, I think people who read the Bible will sometimes have to look for God. Job said, *"If I could find Him, I'd have some argument with Him. If I could find Him, I looked to the left, no God. Look to my right, no God. Before me, no God. Behind me, no God."* But then he said, *"You know what? Even though I can't find Him, He knows the way that I take"* (Job 23:3-5). That's for somebody who thinks God has forgotten. He told me to

How to Defeat Discouragement

tell you, *"I know where you are, when you are, and how you are. Don't worry about what I know. I know it all from the beginning to the ending, you just trust me."*

When you can't find God, it matters what you say about God. Job said, *"Though He slay me, yet will I trust in Him"* (Job 13:15). You know what he was doing? He was saying, *"I'm going to watch my mouth in this situation."* You might not feel well right now, but watch your mouth because the power of life and death is in your tongue (Proverbs 18:21). You've got to say, Lord, *"I'm going to watch my mouth while I'm going through this valley."* That does not mean you get an opportunity to just voice all of your feelings and all of your opinions. If it's not in the word of God, shut your mouth.

How do you fight discouragement? Here are three things on how you can defeat it.

Have Perpetual Gratefulness

Number one, you must have perpetual gratefulness, that means thankfulness. In 1 Corinthians 15:51, Paul said, *"Behold, I show you a mystery; We shall not all sleep, but we shall all be changed."* So, he was telling them that there was hope in what seemed to be the end. You know, when we start talking about when they called my name and I can't answer. When my bed becomes my cooling board and my sheets become my winding covers. You know how the old saints used to talk.

He said, *"When it looks like you've come to the end, it's really a new beginning."* He said, *"I'm trying to show you a mystery."* Some people think it's the end, but the Lord told me to tell you, *"It's only the beginning. He's getting ready to do something different, something new."* Isaiah 43:19 says it this way, *"Behold, I do a new thing now it shall spring forth; shall you not know it? I'll make a way in the wilderness, and I'll be water in dry places."* Somebody thinks they're at the end of the rope, but God said, *"No, I tied a knot and with the knot. You'll be able to hang on in there and the breakthrough is coming."* He said, *"Behold, I'm showing you a mystery that death does not have the final say."* He said in 1 Corinthians 15:55-56, *"Oh death, where is your sting? Oh grave, where is your victory? The sting of death is sin and the strength of sin is the law."* We just need to know that Jesus paid it all. Sometimes I still mess up, but I'm so glad that Jesus paid it all. He said, *"I'm faithful and just to forgive you of all your sins and cleanse you of all of your unrighteousness* (1 John 1:9). Our God is still working on me. He's working on you too.

After all of this, in verse 57, Paul said, *"But thanks be to God..."* He's saying, *"Even though I know it looks like an end, I've still got thanks. Even though it might be hard right now, I've still got thanks. Even though you may not be able to figure it out right now, I've still got thanks."* I just remember what he wrote over in 1 Thessalonians 5:18, where he said, *"In everything give thanks..."* Notice he didn't say, *"For everything give thanks,"* but he said, *"In everything give thanks."* There is a difference. I don't give thanks for sickness, but I can give thanks in sickness. I don't give thanks that something is going awry, but I can give thanks in that which is going awry. I can bless the Lord at all times, and His praise shall continually be in my mouth. I've got gratefulness. Why? Because that is access into His presence. Psalm 100:4 says, *"Enter into his gates with thanksgiving, and into his courts with praise: be thankful unto him, and bless his name."* You can't come in here downtrodden and beat down. You've got to come in here with praises on your lips because you're coming to get into His presence. This word, 'but' is a transition word. It means that whatever happened before it has been canceled.

How to Defeat Discouragement

It's a fact, but he says, *"Here comes the truth."* You can say, *"I'm sick,"* and that's a fact, but the truth is He's a healer. You can say, *"My money might be funny, and my change might be strange,"* and that's a fact, but Philippians 4:19 says, *"And my God will supply all of my needs according to his riches in glory in Christ Jesus."* That's the truth. So, I've got to discern between what's fact and what's truth. When I look at my life, I begin to discern when he said, 'but' that's a transition, and God is moving me from one thing to another thing. It's like a trapeze; you know in the trapeze they have to get to one and then they let go of one turn to grab the other. But there's a moment where they don't have anything, nothing to support flesh. I'm reaching for something, but it isn't there yet.

Somebody is in the midst of a transition. You're not where you were, but you're not where you will be and the Lord said, *"But thanks be to God."* I'm not where I was, I'm not where I will be, but I've got thanks on my lips. I might not be driving what I want to drive or living where I want to live. But I'm in transition. God has me moving toward the thing that He has purposed for my life, and I will not miss it.

So, I'm in that nebulous, ambiguous, uncomfortable place. I'm like, *"Lord, please let something be there when I get there."* You know when you're trying to walk by faith and not by sight, and you don't know where your next step is going to fall, and you've got to keep on walking anyway. When it looks like you're about to walk off a cliff, and you hear the Lord saying, *"Walk."* You're in a moment of apprehension and you still hear the Lord saying, *"Walk."* You hesitate and say, *"Wait a minute, Lord. This doesn't look good,"* but the Lord is still saying, *"Walk."* All you can hear Him saying is, *"Walk!"* I know, you can't see your way but walk. I know you don't feel it but, walk! I know you don't understand but walk!"

The Pastor's Pen

Gratefulness is currency. He says, *"Why are you so grateful?"* Because death has no sting and the grave has no victory. This isn't something sad; it's good news. Your mother and your father who died in the Lord, there was no victory in death. Death didn't have the victory, because Christ said, *"I paid it all, I took the keys from death, hell, and the grave."* Now we've got a back door that once you see me leave this body, I step out of time and into glory.

Do you know something? It's hard to be discouraged with a grateful heart. If you're constantly saying, *"Thank you, Lord. Hallelujah, Jesus! I magnify Your name,"* it's hard for discouragement to sit on you. Discouragement just keeps rolling off your back like the water off of a duck's back. You've got to say, *"Lord, in my heart is gratefulness."*

I'm grateful that's why I don't lose my mind. I'm grateful that's why I don't go cuckoo for Cocoa Puffs. That's why you don't look like what you've been through. If you gave your testimony, some folks would say, *"What? You went through all of that, and you still showed up. You're looking good."* Just know that He'll keep you.

Psalms 126:3 says, *"The Lord has done great things for us; whereof we are glad."* Have you stopped and taken inventory lately? My mom had to raise me as a single mother, but when I look back, I wanted for nothing. Everything I wanted, she gave me. I always had the latest sneakers. There was nothing that I wanted that I didn't have because God made a way.

My daddy died when I was six months old, but then I had my mother's brothers and her sisters, and I had my daddy's sisters and his brothers. Everybody had something to say when it came to imparting in my life. You get wrong, and they were going to get you right. So, I didn't go without someone to mold and shape me.

How to Defeat Discouragement

So, he says, *"But thanks be to God, which giveth us the victory..."* The word giveth is continuous, which means when I name the name of Christ, I've got the victory right there. But it's a continuous thing, He does not just give me one victory because He said, *"I'm not only there for your eternity. I'm there to give you victory in time."* See, when you go through something and you pray, and you pray right, as the old saints would say, all of a sudden, a door opens that you couldn't have opened. You know what He said? *"I just gave you another victory."* When there's a way made out of no way, He said, *"I gave you another victory. When a door opens that you did not see, I gave you another victory."* When He gives you favor with those that are unexpected, He said, *"I gave you another victory."* As that old song writer that said, *"Every time I turn around, the Lord is blessing me."*

Personal Grittiness

Not only perpetual gratefulness, but the Lord says personal grittiness. What does grit mean? If you've got grit, what does that mean? A stick-to-itiveness. What does it mean? Because of what you know, you've got a stick-to-itiveness. Because of what you've seen, you've got a stick-to-itiveness. This grittiness is defined as a powerful motivation to achieve an objective. It is a persevering effort combined with a passion for a particular long-term goal or instinct. It means that the grit helps me to keep going when nothing is supporting where I'm trying to get to.

If you're a business owner and your business has not done exactly what you wanted to do in the time that you've been doing it, you have to stay the course. If you're on a flight and there is a storm, they may alter the path taken, but eventually you're going to make it. They may have to go little higher to fly over this storm, but we're going to make it to the destination. It just might get a little bit bumpy, and I promise you, when you're on a commercial flight, nobody says,

The Pastor's Pen

"Where's my parachute? I'm about to get off here. It's getting a little bit too rough right now. I'm not feeling this right now. I haven't ever seen the pilot. I don't know if he's drunk or what. Here I am, riding back here. No, I'm going to get off this." No, what do you do? You put on your seatbelt, and you ride it out. The Lord told me to tell you, *"Put your seatbelt on. It's just a little bit bumpy. You're going to make it to your destination."*

There's a story of the legend in India of a mouse that was terrified of cats. There was a mouse that was deathly terrified of cats. So, he went to the magician, and he told the magician to transform me into a cat because he said, *"If I become a cat, I won't be afraid of cats anymore."* So, when he turned him into a cat, it resolved the fear until he met a dog. He went back to the magician and said, *"Hey, turn me into a dog. I don't want to be a cat anymore."* So, the magician said, *"Okay, you are a dog."* He was turned into a dog, and he was all right, no more fear of cats. Then he met a tiger. He went back to magician and said, *"I know I went from a mouse to a cat to a dog; can you turn me into a tiger?"* He said, *"I'm not turning you into a tiger because if I turn you into a tiger, you're going to still be that mouse on the inside."* That's why he told us that we are a new creature in Christ. He said, *"Old things have passed away."* I'm no longer who I used to be. So, Paul says, *"...be ye steadfast."*

So many of us, instead of being, we've been trying to do. Just be. How do I just be? He said in John 15:7, *"If you abide in me and my words abide in you, you can ask what you will and it shall be given unto you."* He says that you can't bear fruit of yourself except you abide in the vine. You've got to settle down and get connected. I'm not striving to become what I fear; I'm striving to become more like Christ.

How do we know you're holding on? When you say, *"Greater is He that is in me than He that is in the world."* I know they cussed you out. I know they fired you, but greater is He that is in thee than He that is in the world. If God be for us, He's more than the world against us. Be ye. You must believe all things are working together for good for them that love Him and are called according to His purpose. Grittiness.

Positional Grounded-ness

So, there's perpetual gratefulness and personal grittiness; my last point, there's a positional grounded-ness. He says, *"But thanks be to God which giveth us the victory through our Lord Jesus Christ."* So, that means that as long as I'm in Christ, I've got victory. See, there is a creature that is called a crony, and it makes its home in the cleft of the rocks, and it's out foraging for the little nuts and gathering and doing what they can to store up for the winter. But every now and again, they see a bird flying over. You know what they do? They run to the rock. They back up in the rock because if the bird wants them, it's got to come through the rock. I'm trying to tell somebody that you've got to get in the rock because there is an enemy that's seeking to devour you, but you've got to be able to say, *"If you want me, you've got to go through the rock."* If that bird can tear up the rock, then you can have me, but no bird has been able to tear up the rock. No bird has been able to pry open and come through the rock. I know you've made it out of some things and over some things and through some things; it was not because you were so cute, it's not because you've got money in the bank, and it's not because you graduated magna cum laude; it's because you found your way to the rock.

What did he say? We have victory, but we've got to do what? Be ye steadfast. That word *steadfast* means it's two words. It's *hypo*, which means under and *minio*, which means to patiently endure. Together, it means to get under and endure. So, I'm going through. I'm under pressure, but I'm going to patiently endure. What am I doing? I'm being steadfast. My mind is not wandering. I'm not here, there, and everywhere, but I settle down in the things of God, and I get under the burden that is upon me whether it be the children, whether it be the grandchildren, or whether it be your physical health; just get under and trust the Lord. Trust that He is able to do exceedingly abundantly and above all you can ask or think. Be steadfast.

Endure while under. That's steadfast. Then he says, *"Unmovable."* What is unmovable? To make firm; to cause to keep his or its place; to stand by or to stand nearby. It literally means to be anchored. What is with the anchor? When the ship drops the anchor, that anchor holds it in place, even though everything around it is moving. There's an undercurrent that's moving. There's current on the top that's moving, but the ship remains steadfast because it is anchored. He said, *"Come unto the Lord Jesus, the anchor of your soul."* So, I've got to have my soul anchored.

Do you remember that song? *"My soul is anchored in the Lord, though the weapon, the winds may blow, and though the sin breakers may dash. I don't worry because he holds me fast. I'm anchored in the Lord."*

Next, he says, *"Always abounding."* I looked up the word always because I knew I was coming before some students of the word of God. So, I wanted you to understand that I did my study and the word *always* in the Greek, in the Hebrew, and in Latin means always. But there is some depth to it. It not only means always, but it means every "when." So, when I'm up, He's there. When I'm down, He's there. When I'm in, He's there. When I'm out, He's there. When I make mistakes, He's there. When I do everything right, He's there. Whatever situation, He is always there; every "when," He is there.

How to Defeat Discouragement

He says, "*Because you have been given so much, you should be willing to give.*" Always abounding. You know what that means? The word *abounding* means to continue to increase in quantity and quality. Lady Charles and I have been together over 30 years, but it never ceases for me to want to increase in quality and quantity. I know some of you hating, and you don't like that, because you are looking for somebody that wants to abound with you, but when you find the right one, you don't mind abounding for them because they abound for you. They go out of their way to make you comfortable; they go out of their way to celebrate you. It's not a one-sided kind of thing; it's a reciprocating kind of relationship. If you've ever been in a place where you're the one always giving, you can't keep giving and never have a deposit. You're going to be insufficient in your funds. You've got to be able to receive. Young lady, you've got to be able to receive something. He can't be driving your car all the time. When are you going to get a car? When are you going to go to work? When are you going to bring something to the table? She can't be driving your car all the time. When is she going to stand?

In closing, I have a simple question to ask you. Are you an egg, a carrot, or a coffee bean? Think about it. A young woman went to her mother because she was so discouraged. She was distraught and depressed. She goes to her mother, and she says, "*Mama, why is all of this happening' in my life?*" Her mother, without saying a word, went to the cabinets, pulled out a pot, filled it with water, went to the refrigerator, got some carrots, got some eggs, went to the other cabinet, and got the coffee beans. She put the three pots on the stove, put carrots in one, put the eggs in another, and put the coffee beans in another. Waited for about 20 minutes. Then she took them off the stove and put them in a bowl and she said, "*Look, daughter,*" and her the daughter said, "*I see carrots, I see eggs, and I see coffee beans. What is this?*" The mother said, *"Think about it. How did the carrots go into the situation? They were hard and rigid, unyielding, but the situation made them soft, made them flimsy, made them lackadaisical, and now they're ready for consumption."* Much like many of us when we go through certain situations. Then she said, *"Well, what about the egg? When it went in, it had a nice shell to protect it, but its insides were flowing. But after it comes out, the egg is easily cracked, and what's in it is hard."* Some of us go through tough situations and that's how we end up, hard-boiled. Then she went to the coffee, and it had a wonderful, sweet aroma. It filled the room. She said, *"Look at the coffee. It went through the same situation, but the water didn't change it. It changed the water."* I'm trying to tell somebody; you got to be a thermostat and not a thermometer. A thermostat regulates the temperature in the room, and the thermometer only measures the temperature in the room. You go into a bad situation, and you become the bad situation, but you've got to say, *"No, I came to change the atmosphere, because greater is He that is in me, than He that is in the world."* Jesus came to change the world. He bled, He suffered, He died, and He took the hot water that we could not take. We know that He died; didn't He die? But He didn't stay dead. The third morning He rose with all power in His hand. So, I'm trying to tell you, Jesus could have gotten discouraged and said, *"To heck with it,"* but even when He looked like He was ready to give up, in Luke 22:42, we see that He said, *"Nevertheless, not my will but Thy will be done."* What am I saying in all of this? Don't be discouraged, my brother. Don't be discouraged, my sister. Hang on in there. God said, *"Be ye steadfast, unmovable, always abounding in the work of the Lord, for your labor is not in vain."*

Chapter 6
The Wrong Way on the Right Road

Acts 9:1-12 and Acts 9:17

The story is told of an elderly man nearing retirement age who had finished his shift and was preparing to go home. After clocking out, making it to his vehicle, getting on the road, and riding along, his phone rang. He looked and saw that it was his wife, and when he answered, she was in a panic. She said, *"Honey, be careful driving because I'm watching the news, and there's a maniac on the interstate causing accidents because he's going the wrong way."* Her husband said, *"A maniac? There are hundreds of people out here going the wrong way. What is wrong with these people?"* If you missed that, he was the one going the wrong way. He was on the right road, but he was going the wrong way.

The Pastor's Pen

It's so easy for us as people who name the name of Christ to be on the right road; yet going the wrong way. It can be pride that keeps us going the wrong way. It can be anger keeping us going the wrong way. It can be malice, strife, envy, and jealousy keeping us going the wrong way on the right road. While we've got our hands lifted and our mouths filled with praise, we can be going the wrong way.

And what happens is he had the wrong mindset, even though he was on the right road. He was confused, and I'm looking at the landscape of our society and the times that we are living in, and so many are confused. They are being tossed by every wind and every doctrine, following any and everything. They might be with Jesus one day and then they call on the name of Allah the next day. They are confused. You have to be anchored in what it is you say you believe.

I don't want to be confused, and his wife said, *"He was causing accidents."* He was literally harming others because he was on the right road going the wrong way. So be careful, that you're not on the right road going the wrong way, causing other people harm.

Saul, who will become Paul, is on the right road. He is right where God wants him to be. At the time that God wants him to be there. But he's in the wrong mindset. He is a persecutor of those that are of the way. Understand that before we were called Christians, we were called those of the way. Why? Because Jesus said in John 14:6, *"I am the way, the truth and the life. No man comes unto the Father, but by me."* He was letting us know this is the way that we ought to walk. So, they will call those of the way and until Acts 11:26, that's where they were called Christians at Antioch. So, the birthplace of Christianity was literally in Antioch.

The Wrong Way on the Right Road

Privilege Overrules Piety

I just want us to look at some signs to watch for when you are on the right road, but in the wrong mindset. The first sign that you've got to look for according to the text is you've got to recognize when privilege overrules piety. Piety is your devotion to God and the ways of God. But you can get privileged and think that you are beyond everyone, including God. What do you mean? Well, privilege is threatened with equality. See, when you think that you have cornered the market on spirituality and spiritual things, when others begin to make moves that match or even exceed yours, you are angry and you try to remove that privilege from them. You may still think I'm talking about what's in the text, but I'm talking about what's going on in life. Privilege is threatened by equality. How dare you think that you can get in where I am? How dare you think that you can work the same job that I work and get the same pay that I get? You're a woman, and I'm a man. Privilege is threatened by equality.

If you don't believe it, you do know that Saul is privileged. He is a Jew of all Jews. A Pharisee concerning the law. He's a Hebrew of all Hebrews. He was circumcised the eighth day. What was he telling us? I am privileged. And he used that privilege to believe that he was better than somebody else.

See privileged ignores evidence that God is really moving. We are in Acts 9, but if we back up to Acts 2, we saw a mighty move of God that changed the trajectory of where spiritual things would land. But because of his privilege, he didn't even regard the evidence. When privilege finds a threat, the laws change.

For example, there was a time where you could file chapter thirteen, and you could erase your debt while keeping your stuff. Then other people started doing it and privilege changed the rules. You thought if I just raised my credit score, I'm going to be in a better position. I remember when seven hundred and fifty was an A credit score, but now we have changed it because too many other people are above seven hundred now. Stepping into eight hundred, we've got to change the rules now; you can't be on the same level as me. I'm privileged.

Saul said, *"I'm privileged, and how dare you try to come where I am? How dare you think that you can have some access to God without me getting you there? How dare you?"* That's what privilege says.

You can get on the ladder just get behind me. You can live in the neighborhood, but just don't get a house bigger than mine. And be careful, because privilege can creep up on you. You've got the nice house in the nice neighborhood and all of a sudden, somebody passed the house and you don't recognize their car, *"Oh, Lord, Who's that? There goes the neighborhood."* Privilege is threatened by equality.

Be Careful of Moving Forward Without an Update

Number two, be careful of moving forward without an update. I got an update that's waiting to download on my phone tonight. Some of us don't get the automatic download because we don't want anything to change. And if you never update your phone, eventually your phone will not function. And some of us have operated in what God said, and we're not operating in what God is saying because the Bible says, *"You ought to not beg for bread alone, but by every word that proceeds out of the mouth of God."* It means that it's a progressive revelation. I need every word, not just the word I heard last week.

The Wrong Way on the Right Road

Saul's History

Now let's look at this disciple called Saul. If you read your Bible in Acts 7, Acts 8 and Acts 9, we see three disciples there. Three people who are operating under the auspices of God. In Acts 7, we see Stephen, that preaching deacon who is pummeled to death. In chapter 8, we see Philip, the preacher who went down to Gaza and found the Ethiopian eunuch; he was planting. Then we get to chapter 9 and we have Saul, who was plucking. What Phillip planted, Saul was there to pluck it up. Every one of us has some experience with assault, where every time we try to do something right, someone keeps trying to rain on what you're trying to do that's right. This is happening in chapter 8, you've got to say, *"Lord, just keep me in 8 where I'm trying to make a difference in the lives of those around me."* In chapter 7, Saul is holding the coats of them that stoned Stephen. He watched them. He helped them do what they needed to do. He probably said something like, *"You can't get a good wind up with that jacket on. Give me your jacket. I'll hold it while you wind up and throw that rock. Yeah, yeah, hit him. He's calling on the name of Jesus, hit him."*

Some of us held the coats. You know she has no business talking about that sister, but instead of you saying, *"Let's pray about it. Let's go to her and talk to her about it."* Instead, you're sitting there listening. Silence is complicit. If you are silent and don't say hey, *"You need to shut up. I'm not your garbage, so stop bringing me your trash."* Some of us like trash.

The sin has gone from holding coats now and increased to a fever pitch. He has risen in the ranks of sinners but calling on the name of God. What started out small has now grown to murderous proportions. He wasn't satisfied with just putting folks in jail. He had no regard for men, women and children; a little boy out there saying, "*Jesus is Lord,*" and Paul is staying, "*Put him in prison.*"

He's not satisfied that they had to flee their homes because he was on the warpath. They leave Jerusalem, go into exile, leaving everything they've ever known, and he's not satisfied. He said, "*I'm going to pursue these of the way. Give me permission to go and get them, and I'm even going to kill them.*" He was eaten up with his zeal. James 1:15 says it this way, "*When lust is conceived, it brings forth sin, and when sin is finished it brings forth death.*"

Saul is the wolf hunting the sheep of the Lord's pasture. Saul yet breathing out threats and slaughtering the disciples of the Lord. The phrase '*breathing out threat*' means in the Greek '*to breathe of.*' It means that it was his atmosphere and it was all he was about. It gave him life to take other people's lives. Saul was a terrible individual, but I'm so glad that even when I'm a terrible individual, the Lord Jesus can still meet me on my Damascus Road. For some of us, our life's breath was stirring up some stuff, drinking up some stuff, and smoking up some stuff, but he still met us on the road to Damascus.

Let's look and go a little bit deeper. In order to go really deep, you've got to go back to the book of beginnings. In Genesis 49:27, we see where Jacob is speaking prophetically to his sons. When he got through with Joseph and Nephtali and all of them, he went to Benjamin and said, "*Benjamin shall ravin as a wolf: in the morning he shall devour the prey, and at night he shall divide the spoil.*" If you read Philippians 3:5, you will find that Saul is of the tribe of Benjamin. So, you mean to tell me that what was spoken prophetically in Genesis, he is acting out in Acts? Why? Because of his lineage, and there are some things that have been spoken over our lineages, that you and I have to cancel out with the blood of Jesus. Somebody has to realize what is happening and say, '*The curse stops here.*' It won't go on, and it won't

The Wrong Way on the Right Road

affect my children, my grandchildren, nor great grandchildren. I'm speaking life because the blood of Jesus has cancelled every curse.

Saul is even named for their hero, the first king of Israel, Saul. That's where his name came from. King Saul had some issues. He was connected to some occult stuff. He went and sought out the witch at Endor because the spirit of the Lord had left him, and he had some spiritual battles. Then an evil spirit would take up residence in him, and David would have to come and play the harp under the anointing so that King Saul could find peace and be delivered. And it was a vicious cycle. At times he'd be doing all right and in the next minute, he would be throwing a spear at someone. One spirit, one day, another spirit the next day. And David comes in under the anointing to deliver him.

Some of us are the same way. One Sunday you're one way; the next Sunday you're another, and you come in under the anointing and you leave a different way.

Saul (Paul) went to the high priest, the one who had crucified Christ. Now Saul is a Pharisee and the high priest is a Sadducee. They call them Sadducees because they didn't believe in the resurrection. For some reason, they were able to find common ground in how they would pursue those of the way. It's amazing how enemies become friends when they've got a common enemy. The enemy of my enemy is my friend.

Learn Your Lesson from the Dust

Saul is journeying from Jerusalem to Damascus, which is a hundred-and-thirty-mile journey. Some would have said, *"You know what I'm going to let them stay right over there in Damascus. It's not that important."* But his anger and his privilege made him believe that he had a right to police somebody else. He felt he had the authority to tell somebody else where they can go and where they cannot go, what streets they can walk down and what streets they can't walk down, what neighborhoods they can enter, what neighborhoods they can't enter. He felt like he was the big dog in charge.

It took six days depending on the weather. So here he is on the outskirts of town. They can see the farmland stretched as they get closer to the city. He now sees the groves, and he's on the outskirts, and it's probably been a little difficult to be around him since he had not bathed in six days. As he got closer to town, there were probably things on his mind, *"Who am I going to get first?"*

As I read this, I wondered how could he tell who was a Christian and who wasn't? I mean, the only way you can tell who the Jews were is the men were circumcised. Are we doing that now? I'm wondering how he could tell. Did they act differently? Did they act more pious than the Jews did? Did they smile more or speak in tongues while they were out in the square? How could he identify them? It must have been that they acted differently than anybody else, and they didn't care who knew it. Why? Because in Acts 2, when the Holy Ghost comes on you, there was no way to hide that the Holy Ghost was abiding in you. Remember, when you used to try to go to the club after you got saved and folks walked up to you wondering what you're doing in here. You look like church to me. They identify you right away because you are sticking out like a sore thumb. He went and said, *"I know them when I see them."*

The Bible says, *"On his way to Damascus, a great light shined."* If you read chapter twenty-two, it says it was noon. So, the light that came from the Lord was brighter than the sun. The noonday sun couldn't outshine the risen Savior.

The Wrong Way on the Right Road

Let's look at what light is in the scriptures. Light is information. Light is knowledge. And darkness is ignorance. So, he had to be exposed to a greater level of light. He had to get some new information. Sometimes I wonder if we're operating in what was, and the Lord is trying to get us some new information.

"Come here Abraham, go and take your son your only son and sacrifice him on a mountain I will show you." That's the word. He goes for three days, and he gets to Mount Moriah and they go up on the mountain and his son says, *"Father, I see wood, I see the fire, but where is the sacrifice?"* And Abraham says, *"The Lord will provide a sacrifice. We're going to go worship and come back."* So, when they get there, he's ready. He ties him up and lays him down. I'm sure the boy is saying, *"Daddy, what are you doing?"* And Dad won't say anything. He's pulling the knife, and the son is saying, *"Daddy, Daddy, what are you doing?"* He is getting ready to plunge the knife and all of a sudden, the Lord says, *"Wait."* What if he had just gone with what God said and not what God was saying? He would have killed the blessing. So, you got to keep your ears open, not to what God said, but to what God is saying.

The information came, and the light was so bright it knocked him in the dust. Have you ever been in the dust, trying to find God? Trying to figure out what God is doing in the dust of your relationships, the dust of your marriage, the dust of your relationship with your adult children. Everything is dusty and you're trying to figure out; *"Lord, where are you? What are you doing here? I'm in an uncomfortable situation, and I thought I was right."*

When you come to the realization that you were wrong can you deal with that dust? As some of you are reading, you are feeling a little dusty right now because you were as wrong as two left shoes. You declared that you were right, even at the expense of a relationship. You were riding on your high horse.

Do you value being right more than you do the relationship? Are you willing to lose your daughter because you don't agree with the way she raised your grandchildren? Are you willing to be denied access to your grandchildren because you can't get along with your son's baby mama? Why don't you with your privileged self just shut your mouth and just say, *"Baby, I just wanted to call and check on everyone. Is there anything I can do for you? How's the grandbaby doing?"* Instead of trying to inject your opinion all the time.

We need some light because we're in a dusty place. Can I ask you a question? What will it take for you to listen? How many times does God have to slap you to the ground because you're hardheaded? When will you listen? Saul is in the dust, and God has his undivided attention.

I remember when I used to be walking and acted like I wasn't going to listen to my mother. Then I heard that belt and immediately she had my undivided attention. I would say, *"Ma'am."* *"Oh, you can hear me now."* *"Yes, ma'am."*

When would you listen? Now they are there together. Suddenly, there was a bright light shining all around him. It came from heaven to the earth and heard a voice say, *"Now you can hear me. Saul. Saul why persecutest thou me?"* And he said, *"Who art thou, Lord?"* It's unmistakable. I know that is authority, *"Who art thou, Lord?"* What's it going to take? The Lord had to take drastic measures to get Saul's attention. He had to show Saul who He was because Saul had been taught by the rabbis that God no longer spoke directly to individuals like he did in the days of the prophets. They were teaching him that God didn't do that anymore. They said, *"So don't tell folks you heard from the Lord."* They made him believe that all you've got to understand is that what you get

The Wrong Way on the Right Road

now is an echo of God's voice. An echo is just simply something that was said before. We don't need an echo; we need a fresh word from God.

Some Things Can't Be Taught

So, during Saul's experience, he learned that he could hear from the Lord. The final point I want to make is some things can't be taught by earthly instructors, especially those who can't see beyond the end of their noses. What does he say to him? He says, *"Saul, I am Jesus, whom thou persecute, it is hard for thee to kick against the pricks."* What are you saying? Lord, kick against the pricks. Let me explain what is being said. When they would plow, they would have an ox, and they'd have him in the harness, but the farmer was behind them. There were two pointed sticks. The purpose of these sticks was so that if the ox or the bull would try to back up when the farmer is trying to get him to go forward, the sticks would stick him. This prick would keep him moving in the right direction. When Jesus tells him it is hard for thee to kick against the prick, it means the prick has been in place for a while and Saul has been ignoring it, causing himself some pain.

The same can be said about some of us. You come to church, and you get a prick. You just ignore it and keep on going like you have been doing, and it's causing you pain and you wonder why your life is so painful. He said, *"Because you're kicking against the pricks."*

You think you're big and bad enough to do whatever it is you want to do, but you're kicking against the pricks. So that means Saul was having an inward struggle. God was pricking him. He said, *"Those are My people you're putting in prison."*

The ox and the donkey are very stubborn and stupid, but they are valuable. They are valued by the farmer, but the farmer says, *"I can still use them for good, but they must just respond to the prick."* So, two questions you've got to ask yourself, *"Who are You, Lord? Who are You now? Because I needed updated information, I've only known you as Adonai."* In Genesis 16:13, Hagar got to know Him as '*El Roi, the God that sees me.*'

So, it doesn't matter where you are, God sees you. It doesn't matter what you're going through, God sees you. And God just doesn't see you and not do anything, but He's moving in such a way that you can perceive right now where you are. He's moving things, rearranging things, and causing all things to work together for your good because He is El Roi.

In Genesis 17:1-2, when Abraham was ninety-nine years old, the Lord appeared to him and said, *"I am God Almighty."* What is that? That's *El Shaddai*, the God of more than enough. In Genesis 22:14, Abraham stood on Mount Moriah and said, *"He is Jehovah Jireh."* In 2 Samuel 22:47, after God delivered David from the hand of Saul and all of his enemies, he said, *"You are El Salah, God the rock of my salvation."* He is the stable place. He's that place where I can stand when nothing else in my life is stable.

So, who is God to you right now? What is God doing in your life right now? Do you know Him as Jireh? Do you know Him as El Roi? You know Him as M'Kaddesh? Do you know Him as Shammah? You've got to get to the place where you say He is all that you need.

Not only should you ask Him, *"Who were You then, but who are You are now, Lord in the season that I'm living in?"* Paul said, *"What would You have me to do?"* You're probably scared to ask this question of the Lord, but ask it anyway. We are scared that if we ask, He might tell us we need to go to Africa. I don't want to go to Africa. You need to ask the Lord,

The Wrong Way on the Right Road

"Lord, what would You have me to do?" The safest place in the whole wide world is in the will of God.

Saul said, *"What would You have me to do?"* In His response, the Lord said, *"Be led to the street that is called straight."* Wait a minute, he had to be led when he was leading before. Let me ask you a question. Can you live in the tension of demotion? I was leading. Now I'm being led. I had vision. Now I can't see. Can you live in the discomfort of being blind and having to have somebody else lead you? So many can't handle these changes, they kick the prick saying, *"You can't lead me. You put your pants on like I put mine on."*

When we need to determine, *"Lord, can I live in the tension that is demotion, without having emotion, because we are some emotional creatures and calling it the spirit."* He's on the street that is called Straight, and they lead him into Damascus. And he's there in the darkness in an unfamiliar place.

Are you in an unfamiliar place? Are you in that unfamiliar place and in the darkness? You can't see your way, you can't see up, you can't see down, you can't see in you, and you can't see out. You don't know what to do, so you have to hear the Lord and be still and know that He is God.

But Lord, *"I was a leader, and they took my job away from me."* Can you trust in demotion? Can you believe that all things are working together for good when it's uncomfortable? Put on a blindfold and let someone come and grab your hand. You're going to be pulling back. I don't know if I trust you; you're going to try to make me walk into the door frame. We're not very comfortable if we can't see. People don't like to be uncomfortable. If you're sitting in a service and if it was just a little warm, about seventy-three degrees in the sanctuary, everybody would be saying, *"Oh, I wish they would turn on the air."* We don't like to be uncomfortable, but know that God afflicts the comfortable and He comforts the afflicted.

Damascus, when translated, means *"the beginning of salvation."* Damascus is a place where I'm getting set free, but it doesn't look like I'm getting set free. On the surface, it looks one way, but if you look a little deeper, it isn't what it looks like. I'm trying to encourage you by letting you know that it's not what it looks like. I know that Saul has been doing what he's been doing and going where he's been going, but it's not what it looks like. He looks bound, but he's in Damascus. He's blind, but God's going to give him some sight. He's going the wrong way, but God said, *"It is not what it looks like."*

He said, *"Go and you will be told."* Do you know what faith really is? Faith is going forward without all the information. I don't know what God's going to do, but I know He's going to do something, so I'm going to keep on trusting, keep on believing, keep on walking, and when I get to where God wants me to be, everything is going to be all right. And the Lord said, *"You shall be told."* The Lord said, *"You haven't heard in a while, but you shall be told. I know it's been looking wrong, but you shall be told. I know you haven't heard from me in a minute, but you shall be told."* I dare you to walk in confidence today saying, *"The Lord didn't tell me exactly what it is I'm dealing with, but I shall be told. I'm moving forward without all the information. I'm still blind. I'm in the darkness."* Just know that you get developed in the darkness.

I'm a fan of Batman, and Batman was fat and bloated. He was resting on his past victories. Then all of a sudden came on the scene, a formidable foe by the name of Bane. So, when he's thinking about Bane and what Bane can do, he puts on his uniform that he can barely button up. He goes out and Bane is in the darkness, then he realizes, bats like

The Wrong Way on the Right Road

darkness. So, he goes down into the darkness where Bane is, and Bane steps out of the darkness and Batman starts using his utility belt. It wasn't even affecting Bane. Bane gloated and said, *"Your frivolous little weapon will not help you against me."* The reality was that Batman just adapted to the darkness, but Bane was born in the darkness. I was forged by it, and he was strengthened in it, and he beat the brakes off Batman because he said, *"You don't know darkness like I know darkness."*

There were many people who were losing their minds when we went through the pandemic. Those of us that have been through darkness, we had to adapt to it. Bane said, *"I was raised in this environment."* Batman had to adjust. Those of us who have been through trials and tribulations, enduring to the end, we learned to come through it without a hitch. During the pandemic, some of us didn't miss one step nor one meal. Money was still flowing and even got better. We had more money in the bank. Why? Because we trust a living Savior and the darkness does not scare us.

So, the Bible says in verse 9, *"And he was three days without sight, and neither did eat nor drink."* Can I ask you something? Can you go on an unplanned fast? Three days. What am I saying? Are you able to stop doing, cold turkey, what you have become accustomed to doing? Husband, can you stop cold turkey disrespecting your boo? Can you go on a fast with your mouth? Daughter, can you go on a fast with the twitching of your neck? You need to fast. Stop it. Stop being disrespectful. Stop acting a fool. Go on a fast.

Most of us quit when we can quench our appetites. You got an appetite for getting smug with your spouse. You got an appetite for not performing your wifely duties or your husbandly duties. The Lord told me to tell you, *"You need a fast."* Ananias came in the room and laid hands on him so that he might receive his sight. See, a book can be your

The Pastor's Pen

Ananias. A seminar can be your Ananias. A preacher can be your Ananias. You need to determine what area I need to go fast. Am I to bossy? You need a fast. Am I always trying to control everything? You need to fast. Then Ananias will come.

If I want to be on the right road and in the right mindset, my greatest example is Jesus. The Bible says, *"He set his face to go to Jerusalem."* They ridiculed Him. One day, they said, *"Hosanna,"* and by Friday they were saying, *"Crucify Him."* And it's amazing they spit upon Him, but He kept on walking. They slapped Him, but He kept on walking. Nobody had anything good to say, but He didn't let that bother Him. He knew His purpose was greater than your complaints and anything that was being said, so He kept on walking until He completed His task.

I'm encouraging you to keep on walking. I know you feel like you're in the darkness, but keep on walking. I know you don't feel good about it, but keep on walking, keep trusting and believing, and God's going to see you through it. I know it's a burial today, but there's going to be a resurrection.

Chapter 7
God's Example of a Good Father

Matthew 3:13-17

The word *'father'* is from the Hebrew word, *'Abba.'* It means source, sustainer, and foundation. A man is not a father because he is male; a man is a father because he is made in the image and likeness of God. He is a creator. He is a sustainer. He is a foundation. We understand that our earthly father is not the source; he is a resource. Being made in the image and likeness of God means that we ought to operate as our father operates. We call God, Abba Father because He is not just the creator, but He is the source, and He is the sustainer.

Our Bibles tell us that He is upholding all things by the word of His power and by Him, all things exist. He has not only spoken into being, but He sustains it, He is the foundation of it and without Him, nothing shall be able to be maintained.

The Pastor's Pen

Let me just give you some alarming stats. One in four in America are born without a father in the home. This is inclusive of all races. That is 25%. Then it gets worse when we start talking about those that have been kissed by the sun, those that are black or African, 64%. If you're Latino, it's 42%. Then if we get to non-Hispanic or white, it's 32%. Seventy-five percent of black children are born to an unwed mother. That's three out of four. That means there are many that were never fathered but are attempting to be fathers. They have no idea what it means to be a father. You know about your baby daddy, but he may not know what it means to be a father. So, he is caught in a generational cycle because no one fathered him, and now he's fathering no one. He can't figure it out because no one helped him figure it out. No one mentored him about what it means to be a father. So, he's stumbling through it, looking and groping for answers.

Sometimes he may listen to the fellows that stand on the corner that are saying, *"I don't know my daddy and I don't give a so-and-so about him anyway."* If you go to jail and they give you a daddy's day card telling you to write a letter to your father asking him to come visit, nobody will show up because 99% of those that are in prison have no relationship with their fathers. They don't mind writing to their mother, but they never knew their father.

When we come to the text, Jesus is starting his public ministry. He is 30 years old, and he comes to be baptized. This is a significant event in the life of anyone, but it's especially significant for Jesus, for it would fulfill all righteousness. If you look at Matthew, Mark, and Luke, each one of them gives us this account of Jesus's baptism. It's in Matthew 3, it's in Mark 1:9-11 and Luke 3:21-22. We focus on Jesus in all of these accounts, but if we pay attention, if we just read it slowly, we'll begin to learn that there are some things we can glean from the Father about what it means to

God's Example of a Good Father

be a good father. Jesus is going into the water, and while He's going through this significant time in His life, His Father shows up.

So, what do you do when you don't know what to do about being a father?

Show Up

The number one thing we ought to do as fathers is show up. We've got a whole lot showing out, but not many showing up. We know how to make a biological deposit. We know how to be a baby's daddy, but we don't know how to be a father. They don't show up because they have many excuses. Many of us have a whole lot of excuses about why we don't show up and why we do not do what we're supposed to do. I have a problem with his mother. I have a problem with her mother, but that has nothing to do with you showing up.

You say you're so busy. Who is busier than God? He's listening to prayers from around this world all at the same time. Who is busier than God? He's delivering and setting free in Africa, China, Asia, all around the world, and America, but He still shows up. The Father took the time out of His busy schedule to show up for His Son.

When our children were in school, they treated our children differently because they knew these kids' daddies showed up. I'll never forget one day; they called me at work for one of our sons. When I picked up the phone, I could hear him in the background, *"Don't call my daddy!"* She said, *"Do you hear him, Mr. Charles?"* I said, *"I sure do. I'll be right there."* I went to the school, picked him up, and took him home. We only lived a block away from the school. We went in the house, and he thought he was about to chill and turned on his game. I said, *"Turn the game off, and come in here with me."* He said, *"Huh?"* I said, *"Get in here."* I did what I needed to do. I had my scrubs on because I was at work and had to leave work to handle some business with my son. Then I said, *"Now get back in the car."* He said, *"Huh?"* I said, *"Get back in the car."* I took him back to school, dropped him off, and after school, the teacher said, *"I don't know what you did, but he was a different child when he got back to this school."*

I know we call it ADHD; we call it ADD, and all you need is a good old-fashioned whipping. I know I'm upsetting somebody's sensibilities, but when I was being raised, there were some things I just didn't do because I knew I'd have to face my mama when I got home. So, from that point on up through middle school, high school, college, I've never had anybody else call me, because he knew his daddy would show up.

So, what am I saying? I'm talking to the fathers. They need our presence more than they need our presents. You put Nikes on their feet, but they don't know what you like. You're buying Nikes, you bought her a Louis Vuitton bag and she's in high school, but it doesn't have anything in her head, but she got a Louis Vuitton. Walking around with red bottom shoes on, with an attitude. We need to show up for dance recitals, show up for baseball games, show up for football practice, even if they aren't that good. Even if they aren't playing and sitting on the bench. Be there and root for them on the bench. Let them know that you love them by showing up for them.

When we read the text, did it say that somebody invited God? There isn't any prayer in there anywhere. So, nobody said, *"Father, could You come to this place?"* No, He showed up without an invitation. If they don't even invite you, you say, *"I'm not here for you, anyway. I'm showing up for my child. I show up because it's my duty to show up. I'm on daddy duty."*

God's Example of a Good Father

Can I tell you something? If you've got your child, you aren't babysitting. It's quality time. Nobody asked, but God still showed up. Why? Because this was His Son. He may not be perfect, but it's my son. She may not be perfect, but she's my daughter. I guarantee you, if you have something to say, we have a problem. I can say something because they are mine. You better not ever fix your mouth to say something about my baby. Well, they are 30 now, but they're still my babies. I know they jacked up. I know they make mistakes, but I still love them because they are mine.

Speak Up

Now, once you show up, you need to take it a step further and speak up. What do you mean? Well, he says a voice from heaven saying, *"This is my beloved Son."* My wife can tell me she loves me in private. She can go all out to do for me, in private, but it adds another level of significance, when you do it in public. When my mother would come to school and nothing was wrong, I was happy to see her. Because she'd show up, she'd be cute and everybody would ask, *"Is that your mama, Larry?"* I said, *"Sure is, that's my mama."* They would say, *"Your mama is pretty."* Then I'd reply, *"She sure is, I look just like her."*

Speak up because something happens differently in public than it does in private. When I acknowledge my daughter in public, it's a different air. There's something that changes the atmosphere. It makes her walk with her shoulders back and have some confidence. Why? Because I'm acknowledging her in public. You may call her your daughter while you are with her mama, but I want to see if you're going to call her your daughter when you're out there with that other woman. Keep your seatbelts on. It's just a little turbulence. It's going to be alright.

The Pastor's Pen

Four hundred years, God is silent. The intertestamental season is between Malachi and Matthew. That's 400 years of silence. So, during that time, God sent angels to say for Him what He wanted to be said to the people of God. But here, God said, *"Gabriel, I don't need you to say anything for me. This is my Son. Hush, Gabriel! I got this, this is my Son."* What am I doing? Confirmation. I'm confirmed by my father. You know what fathers do? They give identity to their children.

You do understand that we are in the midst of an identity crisis because so many young men and women have no idea who they are because their fathers have never confirmed them nor spoke life over them. Many of us have never had anybody confirm who we are. So, we just modeled ourselves after people we see on television and modeled ourselves after basketball pros, football pros, and when they mess up, we find somebody else we can identify with. There is a constant searching for identity, and they're trying to figure out who they are. So, then they dress this way one year, and the next year they dress another way because they're trying to find themselves. They don't have somebody who can say, *"Hold on, this is who you are."*

This is my son, identification. I've been identified by God and whatever God has spoken over my life is true for my life. You are a daughter of the Most-High God. You are a son of the Most-High God. I identified you.

Not only is there confirmation, but there is affirmation. He said, *"This is my Son in whom I am well pleased."* They need to hear I'm well pleased with you. Why is that significant? Jesus was 30 years old; He hasn't done anything yet, but He still says, *"I'm well pleased."* You might not have accomplished anything yet, son. You may not have accomplished anything yet, daughter, but I'm well pleased with you. If nobody else says that they are proud of you, the

God's Example of a Good Father

father should at least say: mistakes and all, flaws and all, I'm still proud of you.

What are you doing to affirm your son or your daughter? You should be able to say at least these three words: I forgive you. So many do stuff and never think they have to apologize. Here they are in your face the next day like nothing happened, and you just supposed to forget about it. Instead, you should say, *"I apologize. I was wrong for my part in that. I apologize, please forgive me."* As adults, we are not right all the time. I know; you don't like to hear that, but it's the truth anyway. I forgive you or please forgive me.

I'm proud of you. What are you saying? What have you said? Is there still some static in the air because you haven't let something go that happened 10 years ago? Are you still tripping over the decision she made? Yes, it was wrong. I guarantee you she knows it is now, but you can't keep hanging that over her head. You are going to lose her, father. Is the issue more important than the relationship? You are going to lose her, daddy, and then you'll never be able to see that grandchild. Why don't you just have a relationship? Build on the relationship. Call them up and say, *"Meet me. I'm going to pay for your lunch today. I want to just talk to you. I want us to sit down and just have a conversation. We don't have to talk about any of the stuff that has happened in the past. Can you forgive me? Can you find a place in your heart for your daddy to forgive me?"* Because tomorrow isn't promised. So, you'd rather go stand before God and have to give an account of your stewardship over your sons and daughters, and He says, *"How is it that you have not been a good steward over what I gave you?"* Is your response to God going to be, *"Well, her mama!"* No, God is not going to take that. So, you've got to figure it out. Wait a minute, maybe I need to play the game and quit going off on this girl. Stop talking bad about her when you say she gets on your nerves or she is crazy. No, you drove her crazy, so shut up and talk to her like you've got some sense because you say your relationship with her may be over, but your relationship with your children is what's important. Don't care what anybody says about you to them. You have to prove to them that your love for them outweighs what they said about you. I don't care what they say. This is my son or this is my daughter, and I'm going to be there for them. Come hell, come high water, as long as the Lord lets me draw breath, I'll be there.

Share with Them

So, you show up, you speak up, and next you share with them. Inheritance is what you leave for them, but legacy is what you leave in them. What are you saying? The Lord says, *"He was lifted up out of the water and something came from heaven and landed on Him."* So, the Lord says, *"I'm sending, I'm imparting something into my Son that comes directly from Me."* I just wonder, what have you deposited in your children? What are you putting in them? I know we desire for our children to follow in our path because we played football, baseball, basketball, soccer, or softball, or because we can dance. I was in a fraternity or sorority. I'm a Republican, or I'm a Democrat. I went to a HBCU, or I went to an Ivy League school. I'm sharing my fitness, or I can cook. All these passions, you say, that's what I'm leaving with them. But what about God? Have you shared your God with your children? You love sharing your passions. But anything spiritual? Anything about the things of God? Who God is? What God has done? Have they seen you pray? Have they heard you pray? *Do you pray?* I've got to make sure I leave something in them because if they don't have something in them, what I leave for them will be gone in a very short time. I've got to have some legacy, not just an inheritance.

God's Example of a Good Father

What am I leaving? The Lord sent His Spirit and let it abide with Him. The Holy Spirit stayed with Him. I used to have the boys reading through the whole summer. They read from the book of Proverbs and then I'd ask them, *"What did you read today?"* They thought it was just an assignment, not knowing I'm trying to leave something in them. Because when you leave home, you're going to need some wisdom. It's a whole lot of foolishness going on out there. So, I've got to make sure that I put something in them. There isn't a father who may have a child who's preparing to go to college and doesn't lose sleep wondering, *"Have I put enough in them?"* Makes your voice crack. *Have I done enough?* They don't have to be going to college. Sometimes it's just transitioning from middle school to high school. *Have I put enough in them?* You feel like you're running out of time, and now the clock seems like it's ticking louder than it's ever ticked before. Your daughter is becoming a beautiful young woman, and you know the way you used to look at young women. Every man knows that all of your looks were not honorable. You had some other agendas.

Stand Back

Show up, speak up, share with, and finally stand back. This is the hardest thing to do. In order to know what I'm talking about; this is going to get deep. You have to not only see chapter three, but know what comes after chapter three? Chapter four. I told you it was going to be deep. In chapter three, He was baptized; then in chapter four, He was in the wilderness. Let me back up because you're missing it. In chapter three, He was baptized, and He was being equipped for what He was going to face in chapter four. I have to be ready, why? Because I'm about to step into the wilderness, where I'm going to be tempted by the devil. So, I've to get what I need in chapter three. Some of you are right in the midst of chapter three. Your son or your daughter is about to go into the wilderness. They're going to hear all kinds of stuff and if you don't have something in them, they're not going to be ready to face the devil. They better know what's written, because the only way Jesus could make it through the wilderness was because He knew what was written.

There is going to be times when they're hungry, but the Father told them, *"This is my Son."* Then Jesus steps right into chapter four and is immediately challenged, if you be, the Son of God. Immediately being challenged due to His identification and the enemy challenging who God said who He was. The first thing the enemy wants to challenge is who they are.

I'm just a real fan of *Black Panther*. In that first one, when he was preparing to ascend to the throne, they had the ritual where he had somebody challenge him for the throne. He was fighting in this challenge, and whoever would go down and surrender would not be able to ascend to the throne, but the throne was meant for T'Challa. So, he's in the battle and he's losing. Everybody's getting alarmed, but his mother is not moved. His mother said, *"Show him who you are."* It was like when he was about to lose this battle, he remembered, *"I'm T'Challa. I'm the heir apparent. I'm a king's son, and I will not be defeated."* He was able to overcome.

Our children need reminders of who they are. I've got to be prepared for the battle that is coming. You and I, we're preparing our children for the wilderness, because the wilderness is coming for them. Whether you like it or not, it's coming. I know they're cute right now, but they are being prepared for the battle that is coming in the wilderness. When they have people who will say all manner of things to them because they don't look like them. They'll call them out of their name, that's wilderness walking. You've got to prepare them. Your child might desire to attend Morehouse or Spelman or one of the other HBCU colleges to go to

God's Example of a Good Father

another level in their education and somebody tries to tell them, "*Well, because you're black, you might want to just get a trade.*" You got to prepare them for that. When they can hear that, it rolls right off their backs and they still go ahead and they put in their application in for Morehouse or wherever they desire to go, because they've got to know who they are and not let somebody else speak over their identity. Many times, those that try to speak over their identities can't even identify with them. You don't know my struggle.

Sometimes you have to stand back. God didn't get involved. He knew it was an intense battle. I could see Him in glory saying, "*If he does one more thing, I'm going to come down there.*" The angels are saying, "*No, God, He can do it.*" He said, "*Get out of my way.*" He rushed from the throne over to the balcony looking down as He said, "*You got one more time to call my Son out of His name.*" They said, "*Don't go down there. He can do it, He's got this.*"

Have you ever watched your children struggle and you wanted to help, but knew you couldn't? Some of you can't say the answer, because you've helped them out of everything, and that's why they can't make it through anything. Sometimes you've got to say no! Even though it's the hardest thing to say, two little letters. It's hard for parents to say no.

Daddy says, "*No, son, you're not getting anything.*" Then Mama says, "*Come on over here and get it. I know your daddy. Don't let him see you getting it.*" Y'all know I'm not lying. Just come on over here and get it. We'll just say, "*You came for a plate.*" Lying.

I'm just saying, we have to stand back. He stood back. Why? Samson's dad had to stand back and watch Samson fight the Philistines. David's dad had to stand back and watch as David fought Goliath. Jesus' dad had to stand back and watch His Son battle the cross. He had to stand back while they spit on Him. Had to stand back while they slapped Him. Had to stand back as He went through an unjust court system. He had to stand back and watch as they condemned Him to die. He had to stand back and watch as they whipped Him with a cat of nine tails. He had to stand back and watch as they mocked Him, as they ridiculed Him. He had to stand back and watch as they nailed Him to a cross, had to stand back and watch as He prayed, *"Father forgive them, for they know not what they do."* He had to stand back and watch as He hung from the sixth to the ninth hour, and He had to stand back and watch as His Son died. Then He had to stand back and watch as they buried Him. But on the third day morning, He was through watching. The Bible says, *"And God raised Him from the dead."*

I don't know where you are in your journey with your children, but you have to show up, you have to speak up, you have to share with them, and then you have to know when to stand back.

Chapter 8
God's Witness Protection Program

Acts 23:1-11

In the late 1960s, the federal government established a program called the Federal Witness Protection Program. Those that are in the Witness Protection Program are willing to risk their lives by giving their testimony and in return, the program provides the new identity, the relocation, financial support, and employment aid. Witness Protection is the process in which witnesses who testify in criminal trials give their testimony. It protects those who testify in criminal trials against intimidation before their testimony and criminal retaliation after their testimony.

So, let's look at these terms. How do we define a witness? A witness is one that gives evidence, one who has personal knowledge of a circumstance. It is public confirmation by word or example.

Let's look at the evidence. What is evidence? Evidence is an outward sign, something that furnishes proof.

Then let's look at protection. Protection is supervision and support for one who is smaller or weaker. It is a cover or shield from exposure, injury, or destruction. It is to guard.

I'm not talking about the federal witness protection program now. I'm talking about God's witness protection program. You and I are witnesses of what Jesus has done in our lives. If it had not been for the Lord on our side, where would we be? I'm so glad that I'm in His protection program. He's kept me from danger, seen and unseen. When I didn't know I was being kept, God was keeping me. When you didn't see the bullet, you didn't know who fired the shot. The bullet was just straight, had anybody's name on it, but God sent His angels. He said, *"I want you to go out and cover my children, those who believe in Me. I sent My angels all night and all day."* The angels keep watching over me. God has protected me.

According to the Federal Witness Protection Agency, no program participant that fully followed the security guidelines has ever been harmed. So, that means a hundred percent of those that walked according to the guidelines were never harmed as a witness. When we walk according to the way and the guidelines of, He who has put us under protective care, then we are not harmed. It may look like we're being harmed, but God allows some things not to damage or destroy us, but to develop us. Some of us; we want deliverance, but God says, *"You're not getting deliverance until I get development."* Some of you right now, you're stuck in a situation and a circumstance you keep doing the same things over and over and over, and the Lord says, *"Until you are developed, I will not deliver you."* Why? Because He's saying, *"I've got to get the best out of My witnesses and if you are going to be the expert witness that*

God's Witness Protection Program

I'm calling for in the season that we are living in, I need you to get developed before you are delivered. I need you to stop returning to your old ways and to trust and follow the guidelines I have established for your own protection." You do know we're living in a season where we need expert witnesses. He's looking for somebody, that can testify *"If it had not been for the Lord."* He's looking for those that can say, *"The Lord did this, and the Lord did that, and the Lord is doing this."* You have to be able to say, *"I am God's witness."*

If anyone was harmed, it is because they contacted an old acquaintance. The Lord called you out of that darkness a long time ago, and you are still trying to go and date Paul Masson, and you are still trying to get with Jack Daniels, and you are still talking about Busch beer. Some of you said, *"No, that isn't my issue."* Well, then you are still dealing with the bud, or any other old acquaintance or stronghold that has formed a wedge between you and God. But you have to stand in authority and say, *"I'm under God's divine protection."*

Do you know that when you are under God's divine protection you have an enemy? He is doing all he can to keep you from testifying because he knows if your testimony comes up and he can't stop it, then he is destined for judgment. His time is winding up. The trial is coming up and he says, *"I've got to get rid of as many witnesses as I can. So, I'm going to do all I can to contaminate the evidence."* Every time you go back, you contaminate the evidence. Every time you slip and slide, you contaminate the evidence. Every time you peep and hide, you contaminate the evidence. Every time you tell a lie, you contaminate the evidence.

If he can't contaminate the evidence, then he'll do what they call witness tampering. He said, *"I'll make them come to my side and they'll be my witnesses."* He knows how to make you a hostile witness, where you change sides in the middle of the trial, and all of a sudden, where you were once for those who were victorious, now you are operating for the enemy. God says, *"I wonder what kind of witness are you?"*

There's been some witness tampering going on. I wonder, are you a witness for God? Or are you a witness for the enemy? Ever since Acts 9, Paul has been in God's witness protection program. That is where Paul was converted on the road to Damascus in Acts 9, and here we are in Acts 23 and several years have passed, but he's been under divine protection. Understand that just because you're in divine protection, that does not exempt you from trial and tribulation. If you read 2 Corinthians 11, Paul said, *"Five times, was I beaten with 39 stripes."* I don't know about you, but some of us can't take but one stripe. You hit me once, then I'm ready to quit. You know what I'm talking about? If somebody doesn't speak to you when you come to church, you won't come back for six months. You can't take but one stripe. See, you've got to be like a Timex watch, you've got to take a licking and keep on ticking. You can't be a punk Christian. This is not a cruise ship; this is a battleship. You have to be able to say, *"No, I'm going to stand because I didn't come for you anyway, I came for the Lord Jesus. I came to magnify His name and if you never say good morning, He told me good morning when He woke me up and started me on my way."*

Five times, I was beaten with 39 stripes, three times I was beaten with rods, I've been stoned, I've been shipwrecked three times, and I've been stranded in the deep, holding on to broken pieces. Anybody ever had to make it on broken pieces? I'm just trying to do all I can do. All we have recorded is one shipwreck, but Paul said, *"I have not told it all."* See, some of us, we got a testimony, but we don't tell it all.

God's Witness Protection Program

Jumped in Jerusalem

It's been the space of 10 to 20 years since Acts 9 and Paul is still going strong in the witness protection program. So, what can we learn from God's witness protection program and the text? Number one, Lord told me to tell you, *"You can get jumped in Jerusalem."* *Jeru* means city and *salem* means peace; so, it's the city of peace. You think everything is fine and you get jumped. You think that everything is going according to your plans, but you get jumped. In chapter 22, Paul goes to the people to try to present the gospel unto them and while he's there sharing, a riot breaks out because they couldn't stand what he said. He was doing fine until he said, *"And I was come here because of the resurrection of the dead."* When he said that, all H-E-L-L broke loose up. They said, *"No, no, you are a heretic, you're a liar."* Everybody went crazy, and they started mobbing him and were ready to stone him to death. They were going to beat him, but he said, *"How in the world are you going to beat a Roman?"* Wait a minute, Paul, you just said you were a Pharisee. Now you are a Roman. Well, Paul was using what he could use, whatever he needed to use to remain safe. He knew the law and used it for his benefit. *"Are you going to beat a Roman?"* They said, *"No, we can't do that,"* (Acts 22:22-29). Romans had privileges. You know what privilege is? Privilege means you don't get what other folks get. You can get jumped in Jerusalem.

In the context of this text, *jump* means that you think everything is fine, I'm just walking in my divine purpose, and I'm attacked because of it. Relationally, we thought everything was fine and we get jumped in our Jerusalem.

With your parenting, you thought you were doing a pretty good job. Then they get up, grown enough, and think they can say what they want to say to you. You got jumped in Jerusalem. Grandparenting, you trying to do all you can. You are not supposed to be raising them; grandparents are supposed to spoil them. Ministry, you think you're doing all you can for the saints, and everybody has a complaint.

Have you ever had an unexpected reaction to what you were sharing? You went earnestly trying to speak to someone from your heart and you got attacked. I'm sure you have never had that happen. You stand there and you clutch your pearls. Where does this come from? What are you doing? Why? Because you're in the witness protection program and the enemy will influence anyone at any time to come against you. Even though your motives are pure.

On your job, somebody attacks you and you can't figure out what's going on. You're in the program. The enemy sees you. You think, I'm going to be an undercover Christian. I'm going to just try to hide my light. I can go over in the corner and pray over my lunch. You don't have to; the enemy has already marked you. So, you have folks on your job that don't even like you and you can't figure out what's going on. You're in the program. Paul, he gets jumped in Jerusalem and they take him into the castle, and he gets an opportunity the next day to talk to the religious elite. They bring him down and they put him before the Sanhedrin and if you know your Bible in Acts 9, he had already been down there. Remember he asked them for letters. *"Give me some letters so, I can go down here and whip these Christians and bring them back and tell them, you're wrong."* Then when he comes back, he is one of them.

Reproached by the Religious

My next point. After he's been jumped in Jerusalem, he's reproached by the religious in Acts 23:1 *"And Paul, earnestly beholding the council, said, Men and brethren, I have lived in all good conscience before God until this day."*

God's Witness Protection Program

I think they took some offense to that. Verse 2 says, *"And the high priest Ananias commanded them that stood by him to smite him in the mouth."* In the church and you are hitting me. In the secular realm, I am maligned. In the sacred realm, I'm manhandled and misunderstood. I'm pulled in two different directions. I can't get any peace in the church, and I can't get any peace in the community. What is going on? When it seems like everybody is against you, he says *"You all hit me in the mouth."*

Have you ever been hit in the mouth in the church? You were just trying to help. You were just talking about what the Lord put on your heart to do. He laid it upon me and told me to say it in open service, I okayed it with the Pastor, and they told me to sit down. They hit me in my mouth.

But look at it, notice when he was in the world, nobody hit him in the mouth; they mobbed, but they didn't hit him. They were trying to get to him, but they couldn't. Why? Because he is in the program. But when he got in the church, they hit him in the mouth. Why is the church attack more violent than the world's attack? Both of them are violent, but it appears the church is worse. They double teamed him. He did not speak to them who stood by, but still the high priest commanded them that stood by to smite him in the mouth. *"All y'all slap him. Do something to him. Whoop him!"*

Then in verse 3 said Paul unto him, *"...God shall smite thee, thou whited wall..."* The attack. The response. But God told me to tell you, *"You are still in His program."* Even though you've been attacked. Even though they've come against you. He said my plan will not be thwarted. It shall come to pass for your life. Whatever God has said. Even though it may be delayed, it will not be denied. Some of us worried about getting hit in the mouth. What you need to worry about is your reaction to getting hit in the mouth, because some of us may say, *"You hit me, and I'm going to forget I'm saved."*

You can get hit in the mouth at work, school, and even from extended family. When you go to the family reunion, somebody has something to say.

Reproached by the religions and after being hit in the mouth, I get jailed for Jesus. Paul is thrown in jail. Then Paul said, *"...thou whited wall: for sittest thou to judge me after the law, and commandest me to be smitten contrary to the law? And they that stood by said, Revilest thou God's high priest? Then said Paul, I wist not, brethren, that he was the high priest: for it is written, Thou shalt not speak evil of the ruler of thy people."* All of this is going on while Paul's standing there with his mouth bleeding and his lips swelling. He cried out, *"I'm a Pharisee. I am in the hopes of the resurrection of the dead. I am called in question."* Then all of a sudden, he creates an outcry amongst them.

So now, they're at odds. If you're at odds, you'll forget about me. So, it was such a contention in the church that they both were saying, *"Paul can come over here with us."* The other one said, *"We're going to kill him."* They were about to pull him apart.

Worry is being pulled in two different directions at the same time. Some of us are worried right now, and 92% of what you worry about is never going to happen anyway. So, why worry about it? Jesus said, *"Why are you worrying? Your imagination is taking you places that you will never ever go."* What are you supposed to do then? You're supposed to rest in the Lord and follow His command as outlined in Proverbs 3:5, *"Trust in the Lord with all that heart, lean not into your own understanding in all of your ways acknowledge Him. Allow Him to direct your path."*

So, Paul ended up in jail and all I was doing was talking about Jesus. The Bible says in verse 11, *"And the night following the Lord stood by him, and said, Be of good cheer,*

God's Witness Protection Program

Paul..." So, I've had 24 hours in a jail cell, and I need to be of good cheer? This is where your ability to trust the Lord comes in. You have to realize He is greater than any force that comes against you, and He is protecting you because you are in His witness protection program.

Some of us are in jail right now, not a physical one, but a mental one. You allow other people to build the walls, and you put the bars on. What do you mean? When you don't set boundaries, you allow people to invade your space with no repercussions. You need to learn how to speak up for yourself and tell them, *"This is what I will not tolerate, and you're not going to talk to me like that."* If you don't set a boundary, you'll just let anything go. Then guess what? Those people are putting you in a prison. Why? Because most of the times, we are people-pleasing. We'll say, *"Yes,"* when we ought to say, *"No."* We take more and more on ourselves, and we are stressed to the max and drowning because we simply cannot say, *"No."* Stop putting so much stuff on your plate. Tell people no! It's all right to say no. When Junior calls and asks for some more money, tell him, *"No."* You can take them Jordans on your feet back to the pawn shop and get some money for them because I'm not paying any more bills when you spend all your money trying to get you some drip. Your drip has run dry, my brother. It's time for you to sit on your own bottom. Like my mama used to say, *"Every pot got to sit on its own bottom."*

So, I'm jailing myself, putting myself in stress that is unnecessary. Then you're asking God to deliver you when God says, *"You're like Otis, the town drunk. You go and put yourself in prison, close the door, and hang the key back up. All because you don't want to disappoint anybody."* You say, *"Yes,"* when you ought to say, *"No, I can't be there, I'm not doing that, and it isn't going to rest on me."* The other thing we do is you say, *"Yes,"* and acting all sweet on the phone and then your family has got to put up with the hell, because you get loose because of your yes. You complain about it from the point you said yes, *"They get on my nerves, they don't ever do anything, and then they always want me to do something."* When they call, tell them how you feel; I cannot do it this year. I'm not going to organize all of this, it's too much for me and I'm getting too old for this. Get some of these young people and tell them to do something sometime. All they do is show up with an appetite. Do something.

You allow somebody else to convince you that that's the person you ought to be with and you should marry him. They don't even have a man. You ought to marry him because he has a job. But he doesn't go to work. He isn't going to keep the job long. He doesn't know the Lord, let alone want to get to know the Lord. You ought to marry him. What? A heathen? I knew you weren't going to be happy about that one. You ought to marry her. Yeah, but she wants me and… She got one to pay this bill, another one to pay that bill and…

He's in prison, 24 hours, being pulled to and fro, wrestling. Listen to what the Lord told me. He said, *"Think about it. He's been in prison for his witness. He had two opportunities, and it looks like it's gotten away from him. Now he's allowed to sit in darkness with his own thoughts."* It's a dangerous place for us, especially when we think we have failed. Every man, when you raise your children, you wonder, have I failed? Have I put enough in them? Are they ready for this world and all these trappings? Is she ready to deal with that little slick talker? Can she stand up when they say she is so fine? I know I'm fine. Can she stand up on the times when she feels lonely and that she won't succumb to loneliness? Can he stand up when it's time to do what he knows he's supposed to do with the children that he has fathered? Have I failed in being an example of what real fatherhood looks like? Have I failed as a mother and being what she needs? Have I nurtured because our children need nurturing and nature?

Sitting, stewing. I missed two opportunities to witness. The outcome was not what I thought it should be. Have you ever felt like that? Have you ever felt like a failure and that it just didn't work out? Have you missed your opportunity? Have you had feelings of inadequacy or regret over what you said? Paul said, *"You're a whited wall."* What a reaction. Hit me in the mouth. I'm going to hit you with these words. They slapped him and he called them out their name. Quite a Christian response, wouldn't you say? Where were you, Paul, when Jesus talked about turn the other cheek? Paul said, *"They didn't hit me on my cheek; they hit me in my mouth."*

Paul said, *"You're a whited wall."* What's a whited wall? He says, *"You put on clean clothes and haven't taken a bath. You're a whited wall because you try to cover up, appear to be clean and righteous when underneath you're unrighteous and unclean. I'm just trying to understand who you are."*

Maybe in the darkness, Paul had some thoughts of comparison. Peter preached one time; 3,000 souls were saved. He preaches again; 4,000 souls saved. I preach and a riot breaks out. I preach and I get slapped in my mouth. Comparison. Preachers all across this land; he isn't saying anything, and he gets thousands of people packing in there. I'm studying, and I'm doing all I can. They slapped me in the mouth. They won't come to church. I'm talking about feelings, real feelings of comparison.

Well, let me just bring it down your road. She gets married, and you've been the virtuous woman. You did what they said at church, *"I cleared out a drawer for him."* You said be a wife and you'll be found. She was out every night, but she got a husband. She was all on Instagram live at the club getting tipsy, and she got a husband. You trying to be an upright man waiting for your good thing, just going to work. You meet a young lady, and she tell you to your face, "*You too good. You're boring; you go to work and go home.*"

Hmm, feelings of comparison. I see some stuff, God. You're in jail and if it's not feelings of comparison, feelings of inadequacy and regret, then it's feelings of doubt. Maybe I'm not called to this. Maybe people don't want to hear me. Maybe God never called me. Maybe that wasn't what I saw on the road to Damascus. Maybe that's not what I heard. If you get in the dark long enough, I guarantee you'll start thinking about the wrong things. You'll start wishing that you had handled that thing differently. With your wife, you wish you had not said what you said about her mama, "*Lord, I shouldn't have said that.*" Too late now. It's out there.

He's worried in verse 11, it says, "*And the night following the Lord stood by him.*" I'm so glad that when all forsake you, the Lord will stand with you. What am I saying? I'm simply saying it doesn't matter where you are; Jesus knows where you are. Jesus showed up. It did not say that Paul prayed; it just said that he is in custody and Jesus showed up. That thing shook me. Even though I don't pray, you still show up. There are times that you may neglect to pray, but God will never neglect you. Jesus said, "*I didn't lose sight of you because you are going through. I didn't lose sight of you because you're in a dark place. I did not lose sight of you because you've got some stuff going through your mind that I never intended to go through.*" He said, "*I'm here in the darkness with you.*" When you think the Lord has forsaken you, that's His best opportunity to show up for you. That's when He opens doors. That's when He makes ways. That's when He gives strength. That's when He gives hope. That's when He gives peace. Why? Because I thought it was over, He said, "*It has just begun.*"

God's Witness Protection Program

What did He say? He said, *"Be of good cheer, Paul."* Why does He have to say that? Jesus doesn't just say stuff to be saying it. So that means He's saying it because He's trying to quiet the storm within Paul. So, every now and again, I need Him to say something that's going to help quiet the storm that is on the inside of me. The wind can be raging around me, but I need Him to quiet the storm within me. Yes, I'm in a jail cell, but God quiet this storm, be of good cheer.

Yes, you heard the doctor's diagnosis, but be of good cheer. Yes, your son and your daughter may act a fool, but be of good cheer. Things may not be like you're wanting to be right now but be of good cheer. Jesus said, *"Be of good cheer."*

In Matthew 9:2, He said, *"...Son, be of good cheer; thy sins be forgiven thee."* In Matthew 9:22, the woman with the issue of blood came and grabbed the hem of His garment, and He said, *"...Daughter, be of good comfort* (cheer); *thy faith hath made thee whole."* In Matthew 14:27, Jesus said unto the disciples that were frightened and ready to give up, *"...Be of good cheer; it is I; be not afraid."* John 16:33 says it this way, *"...In the world ye shall have tribulation: but be of good cheer; I have overcome the world."* Jesus comes to us in the midst of our afflictions, speaking a word of comfort. Somebody might need to be comforted. The Lord told me to tell you, *"He is the God of all comfort and the Father of all mercies."* So, whatever it is you're going through, He said, *"I'll meet you right where you are."*

He affirms Paul's past work. He said, *"You have been my witness."* What is He doing? He was comforting Paul because he was thinking, *"Maybe I'm not called."* But God had to step in and say, *"Wait a minute, you've been My witness. You've done your part, but just know that the results are up to Me. You plant, you water, and I give the increase."* So, many times, we're worried about too much stuff. He said, *"All I asked you to do is plant or water. I'm going to give the increase."* So, whatever we do with our children, our grandchildren, those of us that have great grandchildren, our wives, our husbands, you plant, you water, and God's going to give the increase.

He confirms Paul by encouraging him when He says, *"I'm grateful for the work you've already done."* Not only does He affirm his past work, but He confirms that Paul has more work. We see his assignment in verse 11 where it says, *"...thou hast testified of me in Jerusalem, so must thou bear witness also at Rome."* What was He saying? He's saying, *"You've been in My protective custody, and you will remain in My protective custody, but your assignment has not yet been completed; it's time to head to Rome."*

I don't know about you, but I'm headed to Rome. There are some things I have got to do in Rome. There are some things you have got to do in Rome. There are some things we have got to do in Rome. Jerusalem is in our rearview; it's time to go to Rome.

So, what does it mean to be in divine protection? Psalm 91:1 says it this way; *"He that dwelleth in the secret place of the most High shall abide under the shadow of the Almighty."* Then in 2 Thessalonians 3:3 says, *"But the Lord is faithful, who shall stablish you, and keep you from evil."* Isaiah 41:10 says, *"Fear thou not; for I am with thee: be not dismayed; for I am thy God: I will strengthen thee: yea, I will help thee: yea, I will uphold thee with the right hand of my righteousness."* Psalm 121:5-6 says, *"The Lord is thy keeper: the Lord is the shade upon thy right hand. The sun shall not smite thee by day, nor the moon by night."*

The Lord is the keeper. Jesus bled, suffered, and died. They buried Him, but on the third day, He rose with all power in His hand. Why? Because He said, *"I'm going to go through the program so that you can be in the program."* He protected me and then He raised me up. Somebody knows what it means to be raised from a grave.

Chapter 9
Know the Code

Acts 23:12-35

Know the code, and the code is 2311 for witness protection.

There's a story of Lorrie Anderson, missionary to the head shrinking Candoshi Shapra Indians of Peru. One day, she was looking for a quiet place for her daily time of Bible reading and prayer. She went down to the edge of the river and after having her time of Bible reading, she took up her prayer list and with her eyes closed, she began to enumerate all of the prayer requests that had been made. With her eyes closed and in prayer, she did not see that there was a deadly anaconda weaving through the water, crawling up on the bank and suddenly it struck her, burying its fangs in her flesh. It withdrew and struck again. It withdrew and struck again. And while wrapped in its powerful coils, Lorrie begins to scream. It reared up its head for the death blow and then suddenly the giant snake which was never known to release its prey relaxed its grip and slithered off through the water.

While Lorrie was being treated, a witch doctor from a nearby village burst into her hut and stared at her. The witch doctor could not believe Lorrie had survived. The witch doctor said, *"My son-in-law, also a witch doctor, was chanting to the spirit of the anaconda that morning and sent it to kill you."* The young missionary Lorrie responded, *"If it had not been for the divine protection of God, it would have worked."*

There are three things we learn from the missionary who experienced this.

First, while you are praying, somebody might be chanting; don't let them chant more than you pray.

Secondly, there is nothing wrong with praying because we all should pray, but when you pray, keep your eyes open, because there's always a snake slithering somewhere nearby.

The Bible told us to watch and pray. So, I believe that every now and again you ought to pray with at least one eye open, saying, *"Satan, I know you trying to slither around here, around my children, around my grandchildren, but Satan, the Lord rebukes you. I see you, you foul, defeated foe."* You've got to pray with your eyes open.

Finally, somebody has felt the coils of the serpent wrapped around you. You've even felt the bite or the bites of the serpent. And when it looked like he was about to land the death blow, all of a sudden, it relaxed its grip. Because even in the midst of its coils, even in the midst of feeling the bites, you never stop screaming. What were you screaming? Were you referencing Psalm 34:1, *"I will bless the Lord at all times, and his praise shall continually be in my mouth?"* What were you screaming? Were you reciting Psalm 23:4, *"Yea, though I walk through the valley of the shadow of death, I will fear no evil: for thou art with me; thy rod and thy staff they comfort me?"* What about 2 Corinthians 4:8-9? *"I just keep on screaming though, I may be troubled on every side, yet not in distress; perplexed but not in despair; Persecuted, but not forsaken' cast down, but not destroyed."* What am I doing? I'll keep on screaming until Satan the serpent loses his grip.

She kept screaming and he lost his grip. He had to let her go because the Lord already had His hands on her and just know that He already has His hand on you.

Witness Protection Program

In the last chapter, we were introduced to Paul's experience in the witness protection program. It explained how the Lord joined him, even in the midst of his prison situation. The name of that prison is the Antonia Fortress. And He gave him a word that he had been a good witness, that even though he hadn't done everything just right, God still said, *"You're going to Rome."*

I'm here to encourage somebody that has not done everything just right, though you didn't dot every "I" and cross every "T," God said, *"You're still going to Rome."* What do I mean? He still has a purpose for your life. It doesn't matter what age you are. It doesn't matter what stage you are at. It doesn't matter how much money you have. It doesn't matter how much money you don't have. It doesn't matter what school you went to. It doesn't matter what school you did not go to. He says, *"I've still got some purpose. I know you messed up, but I can take your mess and turn it into a message."* Some of us messed up just this morning, but the Lord says, *"My mercy is able to overtake your mess."* Why? Because, *"I am the I Am."*

When we get into this text, there's some things that we do not see, and then there's some things that we do see.

First, we do not hear nor do we see any commands or exhortations. There is nothing by way of the names of God the Father, God the Son, or God the Holy Spirit. There are no supernatural miracles. There are no messages from the Lord. There are no believers praying. There are no explanations of salvation. There are no expositions of Bible doctrine. But all that we don't see, I promise you if you read the text, you do see the hand of God.

It is much like the book of Esther. Esther never mentions God directly, but you do see God moving indirectly. Haman being hanged on the very gallows that he created for Mordecai; that's the hand of God.

I'm talking to somebody who has ever seen God turn a situation in your favor. Where the enemy thought, he was going to get you and put you down. He thought, *"They aren't going to ever get up again,"* but God, somehow in some way, made a way out of no way. He gave you water in dry places. Gave you strength in the midst of your weakness. Gave you vision when you could not see. Our God is able.

There Is a Plot Against You

So, what do we need to know when we're talking about the witness protection program? The first and foremost thing we need to know is that there is a plot against you. Just because you name the name of Christ, there's a plot against you. You called on His name a long time ago. He picked you up, He turned you around, He put your feet on solid ground, and you thought because of that, *"I'm exempt from any kind of attack,"* but that is not the truth. Just because you do call on the name of Christ, the devil will do his best to attack you. You will be attacked because you stepped out of darkness into the marvelous light and by doing so, you became an instant target.

Being a target may look a certain way to some people and another way for others. The devil believes that because we are in the light, we have just become an easy target. What the devil fails to realize is that Jesus is not in the darkness, but He is the light. He's not in the light, but He is the light. The devil believes that he can hit anything that's in the light, so that's why we have to have the shield of faith, which you can quench all of the fiery darts of the wicked one, the devil.

So, when you read in our text in Acts 23:12-15, we need to know that there is a plot. He says, *"And when it was day, certain of the Jews banded together, and bound themselves under a curse, saying that they would neither eat nor drink till they had killed Paul. And there were more than forty which had made this conspiracy. And they came to the chief priests and elders, and said, We have bound ourselves under a great curse, that we will eat nothing until we have slain Paul. Now therefore ye with the council signify to the chief captain that he bring him down unto you tomorrow, as though you would enquire something more perfectly concerning him: and we, or ever he come near, are ready to kill him."*

Paul had just had an experience with God. He had just got a word from God, *"You are going to Rome, Paul."* But Paul had no idea that in the midst of that promise there were going to be problems. He had no idea that somebody was plotting against him. When we come to church and we hear the word of God and we study the word of God and we grab a hold of the promises of God, we still have to know that there are going to be problems. There are going to be some things that come up that you didn't expect to come up. You have to be able to say, *"Lord, I still believe. You told me you are going to take me to Rome, so I still believe I'm going to Rome. Let the plotters plot because my God is still great and greatly to be praised."*

Paul is told that he'll be a witness in Rome, but he is not told all that awaits him, as he receives the word. Some of us only want to go to Rome if we know all the information. Faith is not knowing all of the information. Faith is going forward without all the information. *"God, I still believe even though I don't know what's going to be happening tomorrow, I still believe you hold tomorrow. So, wherever it is I'm going to encounter, you've already been there and God, You've already equipped me for what I even don't know is waiting for me."*

Paul got a word, and Paul put on his shoes. He said, *"I'm not going to get ready; I'm going to be ready."* God says, *"You're always talking about I'm getting ready to move."* The Lord said, *"I've been moving, I'm just waiting on you to get ready for Me to move. You've got to be ready, not get ready."*

Now Paul said, *"...the thief comes to steal, kill and destroy; but I'm putting on my shoes anyway. I don't care what the devil is trying to do. I just know what God is going to do."* So, put on your shoes and prepare yourself to walk into your healing. Prepare yourself to walk into your deliverance. Prepare yourself to walk into your peace. Prepare yourself to walk into a reconciled relationship. You've got to say, *"I've got my shoes on. My shoes are shod with the preparation of the gospel of peace. I know there's a plot against me, but I'm ready."* But I hear the word of the Lord saying Isaiah 54:17, *"No weapon that is formed against you shall be able to prosper, and every tongue that rises against you thou shalt condemn it for this is the heritage of the children of God says the Lord."* Know that there is a plot against you.

Know to Trust Providence

Next, we need to know to trust providence when we're troubled about presence. The word *providence* is a theological term. Its root word is *"provide."* Providence is simply God's foresight to provide. It literally means God's intervention in the universe.

But it comes in two flavors. There is a general providence, which is God's continuous upholding of the universe. We see this in Hebrews 1:3, when it says, "*...upholding all things by the word of his power...*" This means that without Him, none of this holds together. But then there's special providence, this is God's extraordinary intervention in the lives of His people. I don't know about you, but I'm an experienced person in God's special providence. Have you ever said, "*If it had not been for the Lord, I never would have made it.*" You're a recipient of God's special providence. I know we may not think enough of ourselves, but God loved us even when we were messed up. He loved us enough to send His Son. John 3:16 said, "*God so loved the world that He gave His only begotten Son...*"

Know to trust providence that God's hand can move through any means He desires. Trust providence that even when you are troubled about his presence. Job said, "*If I could find Him, I looked to the left I looked to the right I looked before me I looked behind; I couldn't see him; but if I could find Him, I'd have some argument in my mouth.*" It might have been good that he didn't find Him, but God says, "*I've been here all the time.*" When you're in a test, the teacher doesn't say anything, but they're always present. I'm so glad that our teacher is always present even in stressful times, He's a very present help in the time of trouble.

Trust providence when you're troubled about presence because information comes from an unexpected source. Look at verse 16, "*And when Paul's sister's son heard of their lying-in wait, he went and entered into the castle, and told Paul.*" I just wondered why we have never heard anything about Paul having a nephew. We don't know anything about his sister, but right when we need the information, God provides. Hear me, right when you need it, you will receive it. God will make sure that nothing sneaks up on you. He will not do a thing except He first reveals it unto the prophets. The information you need to go forward you will have it when it's time to move forward.

The nephew just happened to hear what they were saying. I just wonder, if I use my sanctified imagination, in Ecclesiastes 10:20 says, "*Curse not the king, no not in thy thought; and curse not the rich in thy bedchamber: for a bird of the air shall carry the voice, and that which hath wings shall tell the matter.*" Be careful what you say because you don't know if you are talking to a bird or not. What am I saying? I can guarantee you one of the forty men down at the local pub had him a few drinks and got to talking about Paul. He said "*There's an apostle in town and we are going to kill him, there's going to be about forty-five of us.*" Paul's nephew said, "*Uh-huh, what's his name?*" "*They call him Paul, and we going to get him tomorrow about this time, he'll be dead.*" I'm just using my sanctified imagination. God will put you in the right place, and folks don't even know who they're talking to and they will tell you everything you need to know. That's what witness protection is all about.

We see in the scripture that forty of them said, "*We're not going to eat and we're not going drink until we kill him.*" Don't miss it, they said, "*We are not going to eat, we are not going to drink until we kill him, so bring him tomorrow.*" They wanted to hurry and get this done because it appeared they didn't want to miss a meal. Bring him down tomorrow. It's already twelve; we stopped eating after twelve anyway. That's just funny because Jesus, one, could fast forty days, but the forty men couldn't fast one day.

What do we have here? We have these forty plus men who they call Jewish terrorists. They call them dagger carriers. When there was an assignment to kill, they would show up at a feast where there were a lot of people and then they would pull their concealed weapon out to do damage. They would stab and disappear in the midst of the crowd as if they had never done anything, assassins. There are some assassins out there.

What amazes is that they were able to get the Jewish leadership to agree with them. They went to the preachers and said, *"We're getting ready to kill a man,"* and nobody rebuked them. Why? Because they gave big tithes to the church. They didn't rebuke them because they could sing in the choir. They didn't rebuke them because they were a musician. They didn't rebuke them because they were there when they laid the cornerstone for the temple. They did not rebuke them. They were the leaders of the church, and they knew what the commandments were; the sixth commandment said, "Thou shalt not murder," yet they did nothing. They know the Word and could quote Psalm 23 verbatim. They knew the psalm, but what we need to realize is that Paul knew the Shepherd. Do you know the Shepherd?

I just find that amazing. His nephew came and said, *"I got something to tell you."* *"What's going on, nephew?"* Because at that time, they would let the family members come and bring them a plate of food, and they would feed them while they were incarcerated. *"Uncle, I got something else to tell you with this plate of food. They are trying to kill you. They mean to kill you tomorrow about this time, and they plan to do it under the guise of bringing you down before the magistrates."*

So, Paul has this providence working in his favor and then the chief captain. The chief captain is a tribune of over 600 to a thousand soldiers; his name is Claudius Lysias. He is the same one that earlier in Acts 23 wanted to flog Paul into a confession that he did something wrong, but now God has providentially turned his heart towards Paul instead of working against Paul.

I know your supervisor gets on your last nerve, but you've got to know the heart of the king is in the hands of the Lord. He directs which way it takes and He'll fix it for you. God can turn somebody who was previously against you in your favor. He said, "*I learned he was a Roman citizen.*" Privilege always plays the privilege card. If privilege plays the privilege card, you and I are privileged in God; therefore, I play the privilege card. I'm a child of the King, and I'm going to play that card every time I get a chance.

So, know that there's a plot against you. Know to trust providence when you're troubled about presence.

God Will Send Help

Next, we need to know that God will give you the help you need when you need it. In verses 23-24, we see how He sent help for Paul, "*And he called unto him two centurions, saying, Make ready two hundred soldiers to go to Caesarea, and horsemen threescore and ten, and spearmen two hundred, at the third hour of the night; And provide them beasts, that they may set Paul on, and bring him safe unto Felix the governor.*" Now wait a minute, I don't want you to miss this. There were forty men against Paul, but God sent 470 soldiers to guard Paul. Do you realize that there were only one thousand soldiers there to protect the people of the town, but He instructed that 47 percent of the centurion forces go with Paul to protect him?

Elijah told his servants in 2 Kings 6:16, "*...Those who are with us are more than those who are with them.*" He said, "*I know you can't see it but there's more working with you than you know about.*" When you're out on that road driving that truck and the enemy looks like he might make you fall asleep and put you in the ditch, God sent some angels. He said, "*I *sent 470 to watch over you so you won't end up in a ditch, and make it back home safely to your family."* I'm in the witness protection program and God's got my back.

In Psalm 3:1, the psalmist said, *"Lord, how are they increased that trouble me."* Don't you understand that you've got to say, *"God, I'm so grateful that angels are encamped all around me."*

Four hundred and seventy, Paul went from having no horse to having two horses, so if he gets tired on one horse, he can get on another. I'm just talking to somebody who has experienced the favor of God. One car broke down, and God gave you a second one. I'm just trying to show you that God will provide and take care of your needs. He has 470 soldiers to protect him and escort him out of the city. They were instructed to come about the third hour of the night. The third hour of the night is nine o'clock. This gave them an advantage of being under the cover of darkness while they left the city. The streets of the city are empty when it gets dark. This allowed Paul to leave without anybody knowing what was going on. So, God says, *"I'll hide you in plain sight."*

The psalmist in Psalm 27:5 said, *"In the pavilion of his secret place he shall hide me."* Every now and again, we all need to be hidden in plain sight. God, I'm here on this job and there are some devils all around me; hide me, Jesus.

Under the cover of darkness, understand at nine o'clock that's the first watch of the night. If you studied the prayer watches with me, the first watch of the night is a time to release anxieties and give thanks to God for bringing us through the day. It's where your future is released. I'm going to Rome because God's got a purpose for me in Rome. So, he releases all of his anxieties. He says, *"Thank you, Lord, that I've got peace that surpasses all understanding. Thank you, Lord, that my heart is guarded against everything that will come to worry me and to give me strife."* That's what you're supposed to be praying in the evening, *"God I'm so grateful."* He says, *"I'm releasing my future because this is the third hour of the night."*

God told me to tell you, *"The streets are clear for you."* I don't know who that's for, but the Lord said, *"Tell them the streets are clear. What blocked you before will not block you again."* If you don't receive it, then it isn't for you, but if you can receive that's for you, because somebody's been saying, *"God, I've been praying this way, praying that way and it seemed like I was blocked on every hand,"* but the Lord said, *"The streets are clear for you."*

Lady Charles and I traveled to Sarasota, Florida, and we could hear the pilot saying, *"We've been cleared for takeoff,"* meaning the streets were clear, the strip was clear, and you are now able to take off. I'm trying to let somebody know that God has cleared you for takeoff.

It's the cover of darkness; it's the numbers that God gave 470 against 40. You do know they were willing to die and they didn't care. They said, *"We are going down in the midst of them and we are going to kill them even if some of us die."* Forty won't stand against 470. That's what God is saying; 40 will not stand against 470. What the enemy has prepared will not stand against what God provides.

God's timing put him in the middle of the night. If you back up to Acts 16, Paul was used to God moving in the middle of the night. Because in Acts 16:25-26, it said, *"And at midnight Paul and Silas prayed, and sang praises unto God: and the prisoners heard them. And suddenly there was a great earthquake, so that the foundations of the prison were shaken: and immediately all the doors were opened, and every one's bands were loosed."* It was in the middle of the night. I'm looking for somebody who said to God, *"I'm in a night season, and I need You to loose the bands and open the doors right now, God."*

The distance from where Paul was to where he wanted to be was 60 miles and they were on horseback. I found out that a horse could travel 60 miles in 5 to 7 hours depending on the weather. So, we are going to say it was a clear night; the moon was shining bright, and they could make it to the destination in 5 hours. That would still make him get there at 1 or 2 o'clock in the morning. So, he had to ride through the night. I'm just trying to tell somebody that you need to ride through the night. I'm riding through the night saying, *"God, I love you and God, I magnify You, but I'm going to ride."* Some of us want to get off the horse, but the Lord says, *"Ride through the night."* I know the diagnosis has been dire, but ride through the night. I know you lost your relationship, but ride through the night because you are going to make it to your destination, if you just stay on the horse.

Two-hundred-foot soldiers, 70 horsemen, and 2 spearmen. So, if the foot soldiers don't get you with the sword, the spearmen are going to get you with the spear. Four hundred and seventy total. You know who that is, 'El Shaddai,' God provided more than enough. God has been El Shaddai in your life. You open the closet and all those clothes you've got in there. Some you can't get in anymore, but you still have them and you say, *"Lord, what am I going to wear today?"* Because God has been El Shaddai in your life. You open that bottom closet and you have shoes stacked from corner to corner and you say, *"What shoes go best with this outfit I have on?"* Because God has been El Shaddai in your life.

Know the Code

They Cannot Curse What God Has Blessed

Next, let's talk about how they cannot curse what God has blessed. They said, *"We want you to bring Paul down to us so that we can kill him."* When they said, *"Down to us,"* they were talking about a place in the temple called the chamber of the hewn stone. This is where the seat of the 71 magistrates, those members of the Sanhedrin court would sit. It was the equivalent to what we would call our Supreme Court. They were governing, but they were also religious. So, it was half inside the sanctuary and half outside the sanctuary. There are some of us who are half in and half out. If we are following the guidelines of the Bible, we know that we can't straddle the fence; you either are or you aren't, no in between. The Bible says, *"You're either cold or you're hot, but you can't be lukewarm or He will spew you out."* You have got to make up your mind and know where you are in your walk with God. You can't be half in and half out.

The assassins had justices from the Supreme Court in their pocket. They became a curse. They said, *"We curse ourselves until Paul is dead."* I just wonder: after they found out Paul was gone, did they starve to death? I bet you somebody got a sandwich. There was provision made in the law that if you are unable to fulfill the vow, you are released from the vow. That's the only thing that saved them; they would have starved to death if they were real.

Code 2311

But the assassins became a curse. Remember at the beginning of this chapter, I said remember or know code 2311. I'm going to show you what I mean by that code 2311. Code 2311 refers to 18 U.S. Code § 3521, which governs the Federal Witness Protection Program (also known as

WITSEC). This program, administered by the U.S. Marshals Service, is designed to protect witnesses and their families from harm when they cooperate with federal law enforcement, especially in cases involving organized crime, drug trafficking, and other serious offenses. The code states that whoever knowingly and maliciously or with reckless disregard for the safety of human life imparts or conveys or causes to be imparted or conveyed false information knowing the information to be false concerning an attempt or alleged attempt to do harm to cause an act of crime prohibited by this code shall be fined or face imprisonment under this code. That's a real code for the United States crime; it's criminology.

Let's tie it into our lesson by going to Acts 23:11; that's where the code comes from for us. It says, *"And the night following the Lord stood by him, and said, Be of good cheer, Paul: for as thou hast testified of me in Jerusalem, so must thou bear witness also at Rome."* The plot was to steal, kill, and destroy, but Jesus showed Paul 23 and 11. He said, *"The enemy has been fined because he was kicked out of heaven. For this he shall be imprisoned throughout eternity."* The plot says, *"I want to kill Paul before he does what God has called him to do."* But Jesus gave him the answer in Acts 23:11 before he ever encountered the problem in Acts 23:12. The answer is older than the problem. God has already said what you needed to hear to carry you through your situation and your circumstance that you're dealing with because he says, *"I'm faithful. I'm Alpha and Omega; I'm the beginning and the end. I've already gone into your future and fixed it. As long as you trust in the Lord."* You've got to know Acts 23:11 and stand on it.

These men plotted in the night and rose early to practice their plot, but Jesus worked through the night and sent Paul 470 to carry him into a place of safety. I know you're wondering how that applies to you today, but because Jesus was wounded for our transgressions, He was bruised for our iniquities, the chastisement of our peace was upon Him, and it's with His stripes that we've been healed. All of us are like sheep that have gone astray, but we know as we looked upon Him as stricken smitten of God and afflicted. He bore our griefs and He carried our sorrows, yet we did esteem Him stricken smitten of God and afflicted, but He was wounded for our transgressions and bruised for our iniquities.

So, today even though the enemy formed a weapon it did not prosper. God sent His angels to encamp all around me, keeping me from danger, seen and unseen. In the midst of the darkness, He sent me the light because the Bible says, *"Those that sat in darkness have received a great light." "Oh, little light of mine let that light shine, shine on me. Oh, God shine until I get delivered, shine until I get set free, shine until the door opens for me because the enemy is putting down stumbling blocks."* But the light of the Lord makes him a stepping stone. He sends down darkness, but God gave me the light. He sent down weakness, but God gives me strength, strength to keep on riding through the night. The night seasons of this life are there; anybody know Jesus died for you. He died until the sun refused to shine. He died until the earth reeled and rocked like a drunken man. The moon ran down in blood. Didn't He die? Yes, He did, and on the third day morning, He got up with all power.

Chapter 10
Lifting Your Head in Low Places

Jonah 1:17 and Jonah 2:1-10

The Bible is a book of lifting. Genesis 13:14 says, *"And the Lord said unto Abram, after that Lot was separated from him, Lift up now thine eyes, and look from the place where thou art..."* Psalms 3:3 says, *"But thou, O Lord, art a shield for me; my glory, and the lifter up of mine head."* Psalm 24:7 says, *"Lift up your heads, O ye gates; and be ye lift up, ye everlasting doors; and the King of glory shall come in."* Psalms 121:1 says, *"I will lift up mine eyes unto the hills, from whence cometh my help."* John 12:32 says, *"And I, if I be lifted up from the earth, will draw all men unto me."*

It is a book of lifting, and in the times that we are living in, every one of us, when we turn on the news, we hear news that is designed to make your head drop. Jonah was on his way on a journey to 'Downsville.' He was on his way down to Joppa. He paid his fare, boarded the ship, and went into a deep sleep. In fact, the only time Jonah went up was when they picked him up to throw him overboard. Then he went down, down, down into the belly of the fish that God had prepared for him. It was a down journey. Don't lose sight of the prophet. As though he's going down, he's going to teach us how to lift our head in a low place.

Disobedience and Depression

First, I want us to see the connection between disobedience and depression. Jonah did all that going down, and when the storm hit, instead of him saying *"Lord I repent,"* he said, *"You just need to throw me into the water."* Jonah would rather die than do the will of God. It's amazing because sometimes I believe we can get stiff-necked like that. We are stiff-necked to the will of God. We'd rather be disobedient than obedient.

Jonah says, *"Throw me in and everything will be alright."* Wouldn't it have been easier to say, *"Lord, I'm sorry?"* Like some of us, it would be easier for you to say to your wife, *"I'm sorry."* Some of us were so prideful and so resistant to being vulnerable that we'd rather not say, *"Sorry."* We'd rather die before we said sorry. We'd rather die before we say, *"I was wrong."* Wouldn't it be easier, woman, for you to say to your husband, *"I'm sorry, boo."* But you're so interested in winning the argument that you value winning over the relationship.

So, Jonah brings himself to a place of depression. He's ready to cash in his chips. He thinks there's nothing left for him to do. I know what he said, *"God, but I'd rather die than go to Nineveh and be obedient to you. So, throw me in and I'll die right here tonight."* But listen, what you think is punishment just might be protection.

When Jonah was thrown in, we see in Jonah 1:17 where it says, *"Now the LORD had prepared a great fish to swallow up Jonah. And Jonah was in the belly of the fish three days and three nights."* This fish prepared for Jonah was a cell; it is a branch of the Witness Protection Program. He has a cell prepared for Jonah. Why? Because Jonah is guilty of the crimes of felonious fleeing, disorderly conduct, and failure to appear. So, God says *"I've sent out the wind to arrest him. You've been served the summons to appear in the court of Almighty God."* Jonah was positioned in that great fish so that he could find himself due to his disobedience. He knew he should have humbled himself and that he should have gotten to the place where he said, *"God, I submit to Your will for my life."* But because he chose to be disobedient, and ran the risk of a felonious fleeing, disorderly conduct, and failure to appear, he was placed in the belly of a fish. The Lord said, *"You have been sentenced until you get back in line. Until you humble yourself, until you pray and until you get in your word. It's up to you."* What is it going to take for your until? How long will you remain in the cell that's been prepared for you? A cell of your own doing due to your disobedience.

Three days. And three nights. God said, *"I'm going to always get My man. I'm going to always get My woman. You think you can do you, big and bad enough to do your own thing. You think I won't see it or won't mind. You believe that you can keep on going about your way, doing your own thing, but I want you to know, I will win and for you Jonah, I've got this great fish for you."*

You've just got to make up in your mind. Do I want to spend time in what God is calling protective custody? Do I need to be protected from myself? Am I causing myself more problems? More harm than good. Three days. Three nights. Seventy-two hours. Four thousand three hundred and twenty minutes. Two hundred and fifty-nine thousand two hundred seconds. Confined in a tight place.

Some of you, it has been three years. Some have been in three months. Three weeks. Three days. How long is it for you? Jonah is sitting in darkness for seventy-two hours. What is he doing waiting? Waiting to die.

Have you ever expected the worst? And the worst was not what you experienced. He expected to die, and he didn't. I'm supposed to be dead. I'm not dead. I heard other people say anybody who fell in the ocean, it was over. Anybody who got this diagnosis, it was over. I should be dead, but I'm not. It's dark, but I am not dead.

I can imagine, that while he was in the midst of the fish, he said, *"I'm not dead. Surely, I'm going to run out air any minute. There isn't anything too bad in here for me to live because surely, I'm going to die."* I can just imagine him taking deep breaths saying, *"There's still some air."* Then he's closing one nostril, trying to conserve air and to his surprise, he can still breathe. I'm not supposed to be able to survive this.

You're not supposed to be able to make it through what you're going through, but in the midst of your trials, God has prepared this place for you. Others would run out of air, but Jonah didn't because God had prepared it. I don't care what the doctor said, God said, *"I prepared it."* He said, *"I'll keep you in the midst of it even when I don't get you out of it. I'll get up in it with you, because I am that I am."*

What is it that God is extending when Jonah should have been dead, but he's not? Mercy! I don't like what I'm in, but I sure love God's mercy because it could be worse than it is right now. But because God had prepared it for me, I can survive it. I'm living in it, and others are wondering how you are you making it through this. I know some folks in the boat were saying, *"Jonah is a goner. We'll never see him again."*

God extended mercy to him. He was preparing to run out of air and believed it was going to be over for him. Jonah went to sleep thinking he wasn't going to wake up. He thought, *"It'll be over when I go to sleep. I'm going to go on to be with the Lord."* But things did not go as Jonah planned and he woke up and realized, *"I'm not dead. I'm still in here."* Where it stinks in here, the juices themselves should have dissolved him. I'm living in digestive juices, but I'm not dead.

So, he didn't die. He goes to sleep and wakes up. Still breathing. What is that? Well, we saw the mercy, but that's also God's grace. Mercy, he didn't get what he deserved. He deserved to die. Waking up, surviving the situation, that's grace. Thank God for grace.

Pain-Induced Prayer

The first thing that happens if you're going to lift your head in a low place is that you must experience pain-induced prayer. Look at Jonah 2:1, *"Then Jonah prayed..."* Wait a minute, let's back up, do the moonwalk to Jonah 1:17, *"Now the Lord had prepared a great fish to swallow up Jonah. And Jonah was in the belly of the fish three days and three nights."* Then Jonah prayed.

Don't miss it. He was in the belly of the fish three days and three nights, then Jonah prayed. It could have easily said, *"That while in the midst of the belly of the fish during the course of the three days and three nights, Jonah was in prayer."* But Jonah does not pray until after the three days. Pain induced prayer because pain demands a response. You feel some pain. You're going to find you something to get some relief.

Lifting Your Head in Low Places

He's already been disobedient. He's already been depressed. Now he's in a bad situation and he does not pray. What is that? He is resistant. He is obstinate. He is totally rebellious. Yet, he refuses to call on the name of God even though the Lord has provided a space for him. But he was mad because he wasn't going to do what the Lord told him to do.

I want to focus on that word *"then"* from Jonah 2:1. We have not heard the prophet pray not one time in this entire endeavor. He didn't pray when God spoke to him. He didn't pray when he decided to go to Tarshish. He didn't pray before he paid that fare. He didn't pray before he boarded the ship. He didn't pray before he went to sleep. He didn't pray before they threw his tail overboard. No prayer, but he's a prophet. Some of us are living this life without prayer.

Are you in a moment of desperation? A *then* moment? Then Jonah prayed. Are you understanding? Do you have pain? See, we pray differently in pain. All the fluff and cliches go out the window. You're not worried about being cute when you're in pain. Your red bottoms might be tossed to the side, your wig twisted, your suit coat off—all that superficial stuff is gone. *"Lord, it's me."* While in pain, we don't pray those Pharisee prayers, *"Father, You called the world to twirl and put the stars in their silvered sockets and caused every bird to tweet. You put the hum in the hummingbird and the buzz in the bee and the flowers and the tree..."* No, no, no. Lord, have mercy. But Jonah didn't pray at all until after three days.

Personal Adjustments

So, there's a pain-induced prayer and after a pain induced prayer, you've got to have some personal adjustments. The Lord told me to tell you, *"Results are on the other side of adjustments that you have not been willing to make. You've been rigid. You've been inflexible. But the results will appear after adjustments are made."* There's an old saying, *"Blessed are the flexible, for they shall not be bent out of shape."* Some of us are inflexible and we don't want to bend our will to the will of the Father, but the Lord said, *"If I can't bend you, then I'm going to break you."*

So, let's look at what Jonah prayed. The situation ignited his prayer, but he did not allow the situation to be bigger than who he was praying to. See he didn't go in telling God how big his problem is; he went in telling the problem how big his God is. We see Jonah's prayer in Jonah 2:1-2, *"Then Jonah prayed unto the Lord his God out of the fish's belly, And said, I cried by reason of mine affliction unto the Lord, and he heard me; out of the belly of hell cried I, and thou heardest my voice."* I want you to see, he said, *"I cried."* That is past tense. I want you to understand here is Jonah praying a psalm outside of the psalm. He doesn't have a copy. He doesn't have any flashlights. He's not able to read the word of God while he's in this situation, so Jonah has to recite what he knows from memory. This just proves that you better have the word of God written upon the table of your heart, because the Bible says, *"I desired his word more than my necessary food."* I've got to get to the place where God's word is what I eat daily.

He's quoting Psalm 120:1 where it says, *"In my distress I cried unto the Lord, and he heard me."* Jonah turned it around saying, *"I cried by reason of mine affliction unto the Lord, and he heard me;"* What is that? He hasn't made the proper adjustments yet. He's still putting himself first before he puts God. Like some of us, we put ourselves first and then we say, *"When I get it right, then I'll call on God."* This is showing that he still has an ego and pride even though he's in prayer. It's possible to be in pride and in prayer at the same time.

In pride, in prayer, and in pain. Why? Because some of us haven't had enough pain yet. Jonah was in pain, but still did not recognize that was not bigger than God's presence. So, what does he do? He goes to Psalms 120, then he skips to Psalm 5, then he skips to Psalm 30 and again he skips over to Psalm 69. What is he doing? He does not quote the entire psalm. He fragmented it, but he is in the Word. See when it comes to trouble, the Lord showed me that in desperation, it is not necessarily the order, but the grasp of the word.

Understand what I am saying, when I am in trouble, I may say, *"The Lord is my shepherd, and I shall not want. He makes me to lie down in green pastures and leads me beside the still waters. He restores my soul, and He leads me in the path of righteousness for his namesake."* Then I might say, *"The Lord is my light and my salvation. The Lord is the strength of my life of whom shall I be afraid. When the wicked, even my enemies and my foes, they stumbled and fell. Though a host should encamp against me, in this will I be confident. One thing have I desired of the Lord and that will I seek after."* Then I may say, *"Blessed is the man that walketh not in the counsel of the ungodly."* What am I doing? I'm just skipping around because I know in my skipping, there is the presence of God.

Don't lose your mind just because you can't remember everything that is in the Word. Just know you have the Word and you're going to declare what you remember. It may not even fit the situation, but you remember. You may have to say, *"I don't know what exactly to say right here, Lord, but Jesus wept."* See God speaks fish. He speaks you, too. He knows what you don't know. We have to remember that we have an intercessor in the midst of our misery.

In verse 3, Jonah declares the dilemma. But look at what he says, *"For thou hadst cast me into the deep, in the midst of the seas; and the floods compassed me about: all thy billows and thy waves passed over me."* Thou hast cast me into the deep, what? You mean it doesn't have anything to do with your disobedience? You cast yourself in there because of your disobedience. Folks get on my nerve when they try to make it seem like it's your fault for what they did. The decisions you've made have made your circumstance uncomfortable, and that's my fault.

It's a dilemma. So, what does he do? He kind of blames God for his current situation. *"Thou has cast me..."* He sounds like Adam; *"God, if it wasn't for this woman, you gave me."* The blame game.

What is going on? He still isn't ready to lift his head. He's still resistant. He's still defiant. He just isn't there yet. Look at verse 4, *"Then I said, I am cast out of thy sight; yet I will look again toward thy holy temple."* What was he saying? He was saying, *"I'm in a dilemma, but I still got a determination. That I'm going to lift my eyes. I'm going to look to his holy temple."*

Do you remember what Solomon said when he dedicated the temple, he said, *"Lord, if anybody would look to the temple You would hear them and You would answer their prayer."* So, Jonah said, *"I'm going to look to the temple."* He was in a fish and I'm sure there was no temple in this fish. But Jonah said, *"I'm going to make this a worship center."*

When the children of Isreal were coming out of Egypt, they were walking through the wilderness, and as they were carrying the tabernacle, they would take it up and would put it up and take it down when they were getting ready to move. The process of taking moving the tabernacle and putting it up and taking it down was called *proceuché* (Strong's Greek:4335, pronounced pros-yoo-khay'.) Proceuché is a Greek word that literally means, wherever I am there is worship. This term is used throughout the Old Testament to describe communication with God, as seen in passages like Psalm 5:2 and 1 Kings 8:28. The term *"proseuché"* refers to prayer, particularly in the context of worship and communication with God. It encompasses various forms of prayer, including supplication, intercession, thanksgiving, and adoration. In the New Testament, *"proseuché"* is often used to describe the act of praying to God, emphasizing a personal and communal relationship with Him. I'm in the wilderness, proceuché. I'm in a drought, proceuché. Things aren't sweet, proceuché. I'm in a fish, proceuché. I'm going to transform this space into a worship center.

That's what he's had to do. The same goes for us. I know your situation may be uncomfortable, but worship Him anyway. I know they're talking crazy, but worship Him anyway. I know they're looking crazy but worship Him anyway. Lift up your head.

There's a dilemma, there's a determination and there's a distress. Look at what Jonah says in verse 5, *"The waters compassed me about, even to the soul: the depth closed me round about, the weeds were wrapped about my head."* He said soul. What it means is that his emotions are getting into this now. Have you ever just had an emotional moment? Yes, you know the Lord, but your soul. That's why David said, *"He leads me beside the still waters, He restores my soul..."* I can be spiritually fit and soul sick. See your spirit man can be strong and have vitality, but your soul man and your emotions have been hurt. And that hurt will bleed over on your spirit, and it can dampen things. That's why David said, *"I need Him to restore my soul."* So here is Jonah saying, *"They compassed me about even to the soul. The depths closed in on me. The weeds were wrapped about my head."*

Then in verse 6, we see where he is saying, *"I went down to the bottoms of the mountains; the earth with her bars was about me forever: yet hast thou brought up my life from corruption, O Lord my God."* He's still reciting and going to the psalms and finding strength. I'm trying to tell somebody you're looking for strength, you may be in a dark place or an uncomfortable place, Jonah is saying, "Go to the psalms for your strength; go to the word of God and drink until you thirst no more. If you need it, it's in the word of God.

He's showing us how he gave up hope, but he remembered the Lord. Now in verse 7-8, it says, *"When my soul fainted within me I remembered the Lord: and my prayer came in unto thee, into thine holy temple. They that observe lying vanities forsake their own mercy."*

Jonah was on the verge of a breakthrough to break loose from what was holding him in verse 7. Then he started talking about other folks in verse 8. He already had a problem with the Ninevites. So now he got something to say about his situation. Don't ever get in prayer and start talking about somebody else. In the gospel, we hear stories of the Pharisees praying saying things like, *"I'm glad I'm not like the other sinners and all the things they never did or wouldn't do,"* then saying, *"Have us have mercy on a sinner this one and that one."* Jesus said, *"This man went back to his house glorified unto himself. I'm trying to tell you something. Jonah, shut your mouth."*

Here we are in verse 8 when Jonah says, *"They that observe lying vanities forsake their own mercy."* That's the reason I'm not going to Nineveh anyway. I'm not going to help those people. They don't deserve a word from the Lord. He was choking.

In verses 9, it says, *"But I will sacrifice unto thee with the voice of thanksgiving; I will pay that that I have vowed. Salvation is of the Lord."* He found thanks in the midst of the fish. In the dark, in the dank, in the smelly; tangled up and tied up, but he still found thanks.

He thanked Him in verse 9 and vowed to do right, *"Lord, if you get me out of this one. Lord, if you get me away from this fool, I will never, ever, ever do this again?"* Have you ever promised God you would do something just to have Him move on your behalf? This is what Jonah is doing.

So, look at what his deliverance is, he says, *"I got a thanksgiving. I will pay what I vowed; Lord, if you just get me out of this fish."* Then, he said, *"Salvation is of the Lord."* Where did they make sacrifices? Did they make them in Nineveh, or did they make them in Jerusalem? You make a sacrifice in Jerusalem. Jonah still did not have a mind to go to Nineveh; he wanted to go to Jerusalem.

I want to go to Jerusalem. I'll pay my vows, in Jerusalem. Not in Nineveh. And then it says in verse 10, *"And the Lord spake unto the fish, and it vomited out Jonah upon the dry land."* Not because he repented. Did you ever hear him say, *"Lord, I'm sorry?"* He didn't repent. He just said, *"I give thanks,"* but God still let him out.

Do you see what happened? I didn't do everything right, but God still got me out. As a matter of fact, I'm jacked up, but the Lord says, *"Hey, fish, turn him loose."* That's deliverance. See, I like the way the Bible says it vomited him out. It didn't say that Jonah was released. Vomit – stinky, smelly Jonah. It amazes me that when we are delivered, we have no course of argument as to how we will be delivered. You've just got to say, *"God, I'm just grateful I'm out."*

A Powerful Demonstration

I know we talked about a pain-induced prayer and a personal adjustment, now I want to share about a powerful demonstration. I want you to look with me at Jonah 1:17, *"Now the Lord had prepared a great fish..."* Now see in Jonah 2:1, *"Then Jonah prayed unto the Lord his God out of the fish's belly."* Now in languages, there are masculine nouns, feminine nouns, and neutered nouns. When you read the text, the word in the Hebrew for fish in verse 17 is *dag* (Hebrew: fish); that is masculine. When you get to chapter two, verse one, the same word, fish is *dagah* (Hebrew: fish); this is feminine. When we see the fish initially, in Jonah 1:17 it is dag, masculine and it is derived when it speaks of the digestive tract of the fish. The digestive tract is designed to break you down. Breaking down that which needs to be digested. Walk with me. But when you get to Jonah 2:1, it's dagah, which is feminine, and it's designed to speak to the reproductive system of the fish. In one verse, it was breaking me down and in the next verse, it was a tomb. So, I was in seventeen being broken down, but when I stepped into chapter two verse one, God says *"Yes, I've broken you down, but now I'm about to give you a new birth."* If somebody is in seventeen right now and the Lord told me to tell you, *"This breakdown is for a setup, for a rebirth. The tomb has become a womb."* Between the tomb and the womb, what happened? Jonah prayed. Prayer changes things!

Even though Jonah was jacked up, when he prayed, God said *"I'm going to transform this thing. It's not dag anymore; it's dagah."* What may seem to you to be a prison or a tomb, He says, *"I'm transforming it into a womb."* We serve somebody who did that for us, Jesus. It looked like a tomb, but on the third day, he got up with all power in His hands and He's interceding for us today. I promise you, whatever the circumstance, you find yourself in, you can lift your head in a low place.

Chapter 11
He's the God of Another Chance

Jonah 3:1

He is the God of another chance. The year was 2021, and Olympic sprinter Sha'Carri Richardson was expected to be one of the biggest draws to the Tokyo Games. After winning the women's one hundred meters at the U.S. trials, she was set to compete but unexpectedly, was suspended for one month because she tested positive for having THC in her system. Due to testing positive for THC, she was disqualified from competing in the Tokyo Games. She didn't try to deny it nor even try to justify it, but it was later released that she was grieving the passing of her mother and did something that she regretted to cope with the pain. This lets us know, don't judge somebody before you know the whole story.

That was not the end of her story. Only God can take you from a setback to a comeback. She was disqualified in 2021, but fast forward to August 2023 where she wins the women's one hundred final to make her the fastest woman in the world.

She ran in lane nine and for those that know anything about track, lane nine is the most difficult lane to run. It's the most difficult because you cannot see your competition. That means you have no means of measuring your progress. Are you somebody that is running in lane nine where you can't measure your progress by any of the signs God has sent your way? Are you doing the best that you can to make it through lane nine? It's a hard run right now, but the Lord said, *"Don't stop running. Just keep your head down and keep your eyes on the finish line. Run the race that is set before you and you shall prevail."*

Sha'Carri ran in the most difficult lane and not only won, but she got the record. After she ran and won the race, the reporters and cameras were all in her face. And they asked, *"Since your comeback, what do you have to say to your critics?"* Sha'Carri declared, *"I've only got one thing to say. I'm not just back, but I'm better."* What I believe she was saying was, *"I've made some mistakes, I've not been perfect, all eyes have been on me and watched me fall, but God."*

See, I can get back up again because I know God will lift me up again. But she, through all of that, said, *"I'm not just back, but I'm better."* So, I want to encourage you, you may have fallen, but you ought to declare like Sha'Carri – I'm not just back, but I'm better! I'm stronger! I'm wiser because I fell down, but I got back up again. There are times when you may feel discouraged because you made some mistakes, but the Lord told me to tell you, *"You can get back up again."*

He's the God of Another Chance

As we look at the history of Jonah, he is introduced to us in 2 Kings 14:25. Jonah lives in Gathhepher, just outside of Nazareth. Nineveh is on the banks of the Tigris River, which is in today's modern Iraq. We get information on Nineveh in Genesis 10, when Nineveh is built and established by Nimrod, who is Noah's great grandson. In the days of Jonah, Nineveh was the capital of the Assyrian Empire under the leadership of King Sennacherib. And if you read your Bible, you'll see that King Sennacherib wasn't no joke. He tried to get people to agree for him to take over their town and their city by gouging out their right eye and cutting off their left thumbs. He said, *"If you do that, then I won't kill you. I want you to do it to yourself."* He was bloody. Nahum describes Nineveh as a bloody city. In 721-722 BC, the Assyrians and Sennacherib attack Israel, destroyed Gathhepher, and kill and enslave Jonah's people. So, Jonah is living in the tension that exists between God's mercy and the mess and murder of the Assyrians. Living in that tension, birth hatred in Jonah. He could not fathom them being forgiven, even though he stumbled, even though he had fallen, he couldn't see God forgiving someone who had done such an atrocity. If we're not careful, we'll get sanctimonious and we'll get self-righteous that somebody doesn't deserve the same grace that was extended unto us. We were on our way to hell, but God sent His Son. He said, *"While we were yet sinners, Christ died for the ungodly."* We were born ungodly; we were born in sin and shaped in iniquity. and without God, we'd be on our way to hell. I'm so glad that He provided a Savior, for God so loved the world, that He gave his only begotten Son that whosoever believes on him... So, all I need to do is believe! I believe that He sent Him. I believe that He suffered. I believe that He died. I believe that He got up on the third day. I believe that He ascended to the Father. I believe that He is interceding for us. I believe that He's on His way back again.

But the first thing I want to tell you is chapter two is in your rearview. Chapter two is where he failed, but we're in chapter 3 now. And I'm trying to get somebody to realize that you may have been in chapter two, but you're now in chapter three. That chapter two is in your rearview.

Lessons from the Rearview

There are a few things I'd like to share with you about your rearview. First, your failures are not final. You may have failed, but it is not the final say, it is not over. Secondly, your failures are not fatal. You made a mistake that you could have died, but you didn't die. Why? Because God says, *"I've got you in the hollow of My hands. You could have been dead, but I kept you even when you didn't know you were being kept. I brought you along because I'm the God of Alpha and Omega, the beginning and ending and everything in between. My name is El Shaddai."*

It's not final, and it's not fatal, but God told me to tell you, *"Your failures and your faults can be fruitful."* When we look at Jonah, notice God never mentions Jonah's chapter two. He gets to chapter three, and it says, *"...the word of the Lord came on to Jonah a second time..."* We're calling to the God of another chance because the word *second* in the verse in Hebrew simply means, '*another.*' I've used up my second time a long time ago, but I need another time right now. I need the Lord to do it again for me. Yes, I messed up again, but He'll do it again. *"I came over, but God, I only came over because you did it again."* He's the God of another chance.

God never mentions what Jonah did in chapter two. Jonah prayed while he was in the situation of his own construction. He couldn't blame it on anybody, he couldn't say my momma didn't do this, or my daddy wasn't there. He had to own that I'm in this situation because of the decisions that I made.

He's the God of Another Chance

You are in that situation because you've made a decision, but God said, *"I can take what was bad and work it out for your good."* God has taken my bad and turned that thing around for my good. I had a mishap. I made a mistake. I stumbled and I failed. I skinned my knee. I bumped my head. But God said, *"You can get up, son, because I still got purpose for your life."* God released him and never mentioned it again.

I was in chapter two, but now I'm in chapter three. And the Bible said, *"...the word of the Lord came unto Jonah second time..."* *"I need another chance God."* Have you ever prayed, *"God, just give me one more chance? I'll do better this time. Give me one more chance, and I'll overcome this thing this time. I know it tripped me up last time. I know she tripped me up last time. I know he tripped me. Lord, I did it then, but if you give me one more chance, I won't cuss him out this time. If you give me one more chance, I won't look like I did last time God. If you give me one more chance, God, I'll make it to church. If you give me one more chance, I'll worship you God."*

He says, *"You can recover and make a comeback if you pray."* And the good news is God won't bring it up again. See some of us are still in chapter two in the midst of our mistake, and then some of us are in chapter three, but we live in fear that somebody is going to bring up our chapter two. I don't want you telling anybody about my chapter two. I wish you would shut up about my business. We're in trouble, and some of us are living through the torment wondering when someone who knows our chapter two will come knocking on the door.

But let me encourage you. In Isaiah 38:17, it said that your chapter two is out of sight. Thus, it reads as, *"Behold, for peace I had great bitterness: but thou hast in love to my soul delivered it from the pit of corruption: for thou hast cast all my sins behind thy back."* Chapter two is behind God's back.

Then Jeremiah comes behind him and says, "*Not only is it out of sight, my brother Isaiah, but it's out of mind.*" Jeremiah 31:34 says, "*And they shall teach no more every man his neighbour, and every man his brother, saying, Know the Lord: for they shall all know me, from the least of them unto the greatest of them, saith the Lord: for I will forgive their iniquity, and I will remember their sin no more.*" Not only is it out of sight, but it's out of mind and then after Jeremiah and Isaiah had some, Micah had something to say. He said, "*Wait a minute my brothers; it's not only out of sight, it's not only out of mind,*" but in Micah 7:19, it says, "*It's out of reach.*" The scripture reads as thus, "*He will turn again, he will have compassion upon us; he will subdue our iniquities; and thou wilt cast all their sins into the depths of the sea.*" It's a place where you can't reach it. It's a place where you can't plumb the depths of it. It's been thrown into the sea. So, what am I saying? If it's out of sight, if it's out of mind, if it's out of reach, why are you still dwelling on it?

Then Isaiah said, "*Well, if y'all got all that to say, out of sight, out of mind, out of reach, I've got one more thing to say; it's out of existence.*" Isaiah 43:25 comforts us when it says, "*I, even I, am he that blotteth out thy transgressions for mine own sake, and will not remember thy sins.*" God not only remembers, but God forgets. You go to God talking about, "*Lord, I just don't feel good about this sin.*" God said, "*What sin? You already confessed it. If you confessed it, why are you still dwelling on it, I have forgiven you, why haven't you forgiven you?*" You've got to say, "*I accept the blood because You said, 'You're faithful and just to forgive me and cleanse me of all unrighteousness.'*" There is no guilt that comes from God.

Chapter two is in my rearview. Chapter three is for me. Chapter three says, "*…the word of the Lord came to Jonah a second time...*" This is God's pursuit of us. God never stops pursuing us. I know we think we've arrived, but God said, *"I'm still trying to catch you. Because you're still falling and have wanderings in your mind and you're still hesitant about the things of God?"* He said, *"I have to pursue you until you walk in confidence. I've got to pursue you until you say, 'God for you I live and for you I die; everything could be gone, but I'll still worship you.'"*

God is Pursuing Us

It's His pursuit. God has been pursuing us, and He never grows weary, nor does He faint. Fellas, if there's a woman that doesn't want you, you might try to pursue her and try to woo her, but she said, *"I don't like your raggedy car,"* then it's just time for you to say, *"Bye."* God keeps on pursuing us. He's wearing us down. He says, *"I'm going to get you past your resistance. I'm going to get you to the breaking point until you say, 'Lord, I surrender. Your love has captured me with my rebellious self.'"* He never faints; nor does He grow weary. His understanding is past finding out.

God's been pursuing us since Genesis. When He came to Adam and said, *"Adam, where are you?"* He was pursuing him. Pursuing us when He came to Cain, *"Where is your brother?"* Pursuing us when He came to Moses after Moses killed a man. He spoke to Moses and said, *"Moses, take off your shoes for the ground where you stand is holy."* God is a pursuer.

God's Plan for Us

So, it's God's pursuit of us in chapter three. But my second point I'd like to share is that it's God's plan for us in chapter three. I'm trying to encourage you that your mistakes have not made you unusable to God. Your mistakes and your mess have not aborted God's plan. Moses was a killer, but God still used him. Noah was a drunk, but God still used him.

The Pastor's Pen

Abraham was a liar, but God still used him. David was an adulterer and a murderer; at least second-degree murder or conspiracy to commit murder or even manslaughter, but he was guilty, and God still used him.

God had a plan for Jonah, and Jonah's assignment did not change. In Jonah 1:1, we see that it says, *"The word of the Lord came unto Jonah;"* then in Jonah 3:1 it says, *"...the word of the Lord came unto Jonah, a second time..."* God said, *"I'm going to keep on keeping on. You messed up, but I'm not giving up."*

Some may have wondered why God didn't just go get Micah? Hosea? How about Nahum? Anybody, Habakkuk? Zephaniah? Zachariah? He could have used anyone, but God said, *"No, I want Jonah."* Somebody God has called you and you keep saying, *"God, why don't you use her? Why don't you use him?"* But God is saying, *"No. I want to use you."*

God is a pursuer. God has a plan. You know what He said? *"You can't mess this up."* It's much like when we were in driving school and the instructor was over on the right side and you on the left side and you got the wheel, you think. You're driving along and you think, I've got this thing. And you have your foot on the gas, but the instructor has his foot on the brake. Then instructor is like, *"You need to slow down,"* and you're thinking, *"I'm driving."* Just then you're about to run over something and all of a sudden, the car moved because the instructor has the wheel. It's just like God said, *"You can't mess this up because I'm in the car with you, and I know you make faults and you fail."* But He said, *"I've got the wheel, and we are going where I want this to go. Even though you mess up, the car is going to make it to its destination. You can't mess this up."*

He's the God of Another Chance

God's Power is Made Perfect in Weakness

So, God is the pursuer. God is a planner. My third point, we need to know that God's power is made perfect in weakness. Jonah 1:2 says, *"Arise, go to Nineveh, that great city, and cry against it; for their wickedness is come up before me."* Jonah 3:2 says, *"Arise, go unto Nineveh, that great city, and preach unto it the preaching that I bid thee."* Unto it. Preach against it. Preach unto it. Does that mean? Well, if I preach against you, then I'm not there to support you. But if I preach to you, I'm trying to edify you. It's the same as you saying, don't talk at me, talk to me. So, his assignment is tweaked. God says, *"I gave you another chance. I'm giving them another chance."*

Let's look at what Jonah preached. In Jonah 3:4, he said, *"And Jonah began to enter into the city a day's journey, and he cried, and said, Yet forty days, and Nineveh shall be overthrown."* And the people of Nineveh believed. Wait a minute, if your pastor came and gave an eight-word sermon you'd probably say, *"That's all he going to preach today?"* But somehow God took a little and did a lot with it. Eight words. And all of these people, they say there were over six hundred thousand people in the city. Jonah preaches eight words, and the whole city goes into repentance. They put sackcloth on the cows. The dogs had sackcloth. Everybody fasted; no cats, no dogs, nobody ate anything. We are fasting and praying. The cat couldn't meow. The dog couldn't bow wow. You better not even moo up in here because we're fasting and looking for a move of God.

Are you looking for a move of God? What are you going to do? See, they had never surrendered to God before, but they believed that He just might move on our behalf. See, you live on what God has done in your past because you can say, *"If*

The Pastor's Pen

He did it before, He'll do it again." But they had no reference; all they knew was that God had power. They had never called on Him before and they believed that maybe, just maybe, He'll move on our behalf. Examine yourself, are you in this position? Are you feeling like this is the day that God is going to move on my behalf? It doesn't matter how much you say, but it does matter what you say.

He says, *"I'm going to take eight words and do something great with it."* Jonah was told to preach the preaching that I bid thee, and Jonah was given an eight-word sermon. This is powerful; there are only forty-eight verses in the book of Jonah over a span of four chapters. In those forty-eight verses, thirty-nine of those forty-eight, God is mentioned. And the nine verses He is not mentioned, He's mentioned in the previous verse. So, what am I saying? Every verse and every line in Jonah's life, God was present. Jonah tried to flee His presence and God was there. What's amazing to me is how in the world does he think he can run out of God's presence? Had he not read Psalm 139 that says, *"If I make my bed in hell, thou art there. If I ascend to the mountaintops, you are there. If I make my bed in the depths of the sea, you are there; there is nowhere you or I could run from God?"* He tried to escape to Joppa, but God was there. When he paid the fare, God was there. When he boarded the ship, God was there. When he went to sleep, God was there. When he was in the storm, God was there. When they threw him overboard, God was there. When he was swallowed by the great fish, God was there.

Just know that everything you face, God was there with you. You can stand in confidence and say every verse, every comma, every period, God was there. You make it today because God was there on yesterday. Be encouraged and say, *"I'm making it."*

He's the God of Another Chance

God's Passion for Us

So, God's pursuit of us, God's plan through us, God's power over us, and God's passion for us. God has passion for us. His love covers the multitude of sins. Songwriter said, *"I was sinking deep in sin, very deeply, stained within. Sinking to rise no more. But the master of the sea heard my disparate cry and out of the waters, he lifted me. Now safe am I. Love lifted me."* While we were yet sinners, Christ died for the ungodly. He says, *"Jonah, I gave you another chance. Nineveh, I gave you another chance."* Brothers and sisters, He's given us another chance. Christ was crucified, and we call the Crucifixion the most brutal and tormenting way to kill somebody, but Jesus called it His passion. He died because of a passion for us. He loved us when we were unlovable. And truth be told sometimes, even now we are yet and still unlovable, but He keeps giving us another chance.

Chapter 12
Are You a Self-Serving Sinner

Jonah 4:1-11

There's a story told of Satan as he was having a garage sale. On sale, he had all of his tools that he used for spiritual warfare against the believers. He had them all spread out on the table, and they were all marked and labeled. They had their prices listed. If you wanted one, you could get it. These tools were labeled greed, malice, strife, hatred, pride, envy, lust, jealousy, and deceit. He had them all labeled and laid out for anyone that would want to purchase them. But as the potential buyer was standing at the table, he looked and there was one tool that was worn. It looked like it had been used over and over and over again. It was a wedge. The potential buyer looked and said, *"I see all these items, but what is this tool, and why is it so much more expensive than any other tool on the table?"* Satan looked at him with a gleam in his eye and he said, *"Well, I want you to understand that that's*

Are You a Self-Serving Sinner

my wedge. See, that's what I use when I couldn't use anything else against the believers. When I tried the tool of lust and it didn't work, I could use my wedge. When I tried envy and it didn't work, I could use my wedge. When I tried lying and pride, when I tried all that, I could try and it didn't work, the wedge would always work." The buyer then asked, *"What is the wedge called? I want to know what the name of the tool that you use all the time is called,"* and Satan looked again at him with a grin and said, *"It is simply called self. When I can't use anything else, I can always use self. Because those that lift their hands in the sanctuary can be some of the most selfish people who named the name of the Lord. Because it's always about them. About how people view them. About what people are saying about them. About how they feel about a certain situation. It's always about them, and I can always use self against them because they think that self is not my tool. They think that I'm not using them against themselves. So, I've tricked them into believing that the things they hear within themselves have nothing to do with the enemy. You know when you hear you deserve this; that's why you ought to steal it. You haven't had a raise in two years; that's why you steal paper from your job."* You begin to justify your actions. Self makes you feel that you deserve it, and Satan says, *"I'm happy to oblige you."*

Not only do you feel you deserve certain things, self also justifies your actions and makes you feel underappreciated. There's a husband out there that says, *"She doesn't appreciate me."* There's that wife that says, *"He does not appreciate all I bring to the table."* You're unappreciated.

Then, if that doesn't work, you begin to feel like you're unacknowledged. Some may say, *"They don't acknowledge my anointing. They don't acknowledge that I'm a man or a woman of God. They don't acknowledge that I'm the woman of the house. They don't acknowledge that I'm the man of the house."* One thing that I have learned is that if you have to say it, then you are not it. If you have to say you are the man of the house, you are not the man of house. If you have to say you are the woman of the house, you are not the woman of the house. And if this doesn't work, then you're unnoticed or you're unrewarded. What have you done for me lately? Satan has you on his radar with your selfish self, and you're playing right into his tricks and tactics.

Three Types of Manipulation

We do the same things for self when we manipulate a situation to get what we want. You know what manipulation is, right? If you ever been shopping online and you clicked on something, it said only two more left. What are they doing? They are manipulating you. They've got a warehouse full of them, but they want you to believe that their supply is running low so that they can increase the demand. It's called the law of scarcity. It means that you will be motivated to go ahead and make the purchase because you think you're going to miss out on something. The law of scarcity coupled with FOMO is a bad combination. Do you know what FOMO is? It's the fear of missing out. You don't want to miss it because there aren't that many left, so they make you feel that you need to act quickly or you're going to miss out.

Then, if it's not you being exposed to the manipulation of scarcity, you get exposed to the manipulation of reciprocity. You do something so that you can cash in on that person's thought. Since they did this for me, I'm going to do something for them. So, you create the scenario whereby you know they're going to do it when you ask for it. So, you are manipulating with what you're doing for them right now. I gave him a ride, so later on, I'm going to ask a favor, too. I need a favor. Just like Satan and his selfish self. Your actions and Satan's actions are no different. Husbands and wives do this to one another. A husband may agree to do something for his wife only because later on, she is going to give him something. The wife is guilty, too. You say what you're thinking so he can hear, and then maybe he'll just do it without you asking him to do. It's all manipulation.

Scarcity, reciprocity, and in this third manipulation trick, gaslighting. What is gaslighting? It's a form of psychological manipulation in which the abuser attempts to control the victim by making them doubt their own sanity, perception, or even their memory. *"Are you going to believe me or your lying eyes? See, that isn't what happened; this is what happened."* They are trying to twist what you know to be right as if something is wrong with your memory. Gaslighters may manipulate others, but there's one person we cannot manipulate, and that is God Almighty. I don't care how many times you lift your hands. I don't care how many times you shout amen. I don't care how many hours you run up and down and flip over the pews. You cannot manipulate God.

You Serve God as Long as He Does What You Want

How do we know if we are a full-service saint or just a self-serving sinner? How do we know? If you serve God as long as He does what you want, you just might be a self-serving sinner. Jonah was ready as long as God did what he wanted Him to do. But the moment God said, *"I want you to go to Nineveh."* Jonah said, *"No, I'm not doing that."* There is a Nineveh in every one of us, a place where you will choke when God says, *"I want you to go there."* Be ye holy for I am... CHOKE... That's my Nineveh. I can't go there. Humble yourself under the mighty act...CHOKE... Pride has got such a grip on us that we cannot even humble ourselves. God says, *"Either you humble yourself or I'm going to humble you."* Jonah got mad, not just mad, but hot. Some of us are hot right now about one thing or another. Hot at your daughter because she isn't doing what you want her to do. Hot at your son. Hot at your mama. Hot at your daddy. Hot at your sister. Hot at your cousin and them. You are a self-serving sinner. If you serve God as long as He will do what you want Him to do, that's manipulation.

You're Angry When God Blesses Others

Next, if you're angry when God blesses others, you may be a self-serving sinner. Jonah 4:1-3 says, *"But it displeased Jonah exceedingly, and he was very angry. And he prayed unto the Lord, and said, I pray thee, O Lord, was not this my saying, when I was yet in my country? Therefore I fled before unto Tarshish: for I knew that thou art a gracious God, and merciful, slow to anger, and of great kindness, and repentest thee of the evil. Therefore now, O Lord, take, I beseech thee, my life from me; for it is better for me to die than to live."*

It displeased Jonah exceedingly; he just got out of the belly of a fish and instead of being grateful, he is angry about the assignment at hand. God delivered him. God brought him out, without a doubt. God anointed him and appointed him. And he still got an attitude. Just like some of us. Your deliverance brought out self and still go to church with an attitude. You refuse to clap while thinking, *"I wish they'd sit down. When is this going to be over? What time does service end?"* Attitude. He's angry because God decides I'm going to be a blessing to the Ninevites. I wonder who has a problem with the Ninevites when actually, you're a close cousin of a Ninevite. Ninevites were ruthless, dangerous, and murderous. That's our history. If it had not been for the Lord, you know something about God's grace.

Are You a Self-Serving Sinner

But it's amazing we can get delivered, and we've got a problem with folks that's doing what we used to do. Some are still doing it. If you aren't killing them with a gun all night, you're killing them with your mouth.

He cannot control his own spirit. What do the proverbs say? *"A man without control or a woman without control of their own spirit is like a city with walls broken down"* (Proverbs 25:28). That means anything goes. And some of us, our lives are like that; the walls are broken down and anything goes. We don't care what it is, we'll try it. We no longer have restraint; we're just out there, a self-serving sinner.

What was God trying to do with Jonah? He was trying to get him to unsee what he had seen. I saw the Ninevites kill and enslave my people. God was saying, *"I want you to unsee that."* What do you do when it's God that's your problem? When it's God confronting you about your memory of the past? What do you do when God says, *"It's time for you to step away from what you've been holding on to in the past so that I can get you to a place of new blessings, new miracles, and new opportunities."* He said, *"I can't bring you out while you're still holding on."* He said, *"These things that you've learned you've got to unlearn. I've got to take you from weakness to strength. I've got to take you from remembering obstacles to being able to embrace opportunities. I've got to take you from the trauma of your yesterday into the triumph of tomorrow."* You've got to say, *"Lord, I'm ready to let go."*

You know you've grown when you see that past that gave you so much trauma and hurt in your present, and it doesn't hurt any more. Just know that you are growing. God is delivering you, helping you, strengthening you, and letting you believe that you can get past, your past.

Listen To God, As Long As He's Saying What You Want To Hear

Next, if you are willing to listen to God, as long as He's saying what you want to hear, you might just be a self-serving sinner. Jonah 4:4-5 says, *"Then said the Lord, Doest thou well to be angry? So, Jonah went out of the city..."* Wait, wait, press rewind. Play. *"...Doest thou well to be angry? So, Jonah went out of the city..."* I'm missing something. There is no way that if I'm talking to my mama and she asked me a question that I am able to go out of the room without answering her. My mama won't let you make it out of room. I'm sorry if I'm affecting some of your sensibilities, because that's not the way we raise children now. These days we allow them to express themselves and if they storm out of the room, we just say, *"We'll talk later."* Then they slam the doors in your house. When I was growing up, I wished I would have slammed the door. She didn't even know how, but I guarantee my mama would have made me take the door off the hinges. Are you slamming doors? That's what we're doing? Keep that same energy while you get the screwdriver. I'm going to see how you slam a door when you don't have a door.

He leaves and goes in the city, and he never answered the Lord. He just thinks he can do whatever he wants to do. I got an attitude, and I want you to know it. You can't have an attitude in my house with my mama. You couldn't even breathe hard around my mama because she'll ask, *"Are you breathing? Are you breathing? Is that what we're doing?"* Now days, parents let them get away with breathing hard, and they'll cuss you out and roll their eyes. I couldn't roll my eyes. My mama would say, *"Roll them again, and I'll pick them up and roll 'em back to you."*

"*Doest thou well to be angry?*" And you got the nerve to walk away. What am I saying? What is that? That is wasted worship. Some of us are so easily angered; so long, angry; so often, angry. You are thinking you're strong because you're angry. Many times, we only get angry because we don't have control.

He said, "*I want you to see something. You are wasting your words.*" This happens when you go to church angry, worship angry, and leave angry. You come in, got your hands half-mast with a weak Hallelujah and a Thank you, Jesus; that is not sincere because this is what I'm supposed to do and say. Routine. Ritual. No sincerity. Then you sit down and fold your arms because we are angry. And when God tugs at your heart, you've got the nerve to not answer. He's tugging at your heartstrings about something you know you need to let go of but then you get up and walk out.

As Long as I've Got a Chance to Talk

As long as I've got a chance to talk, I'll talk, but I am not listening. God has different ways of shaping all of us. What gets me may not get you. What gets you might not get me. God said, "*I had to break her down because that's the only way I can shape her. I had to break him down because that's the only way I could shape him.*" See we can't think that we're going to be in the army of the Lord and He is not going to condition us.

Practicing Religion Without Reverence

Next point, if you are practicing religion without reverence, you might be a self-serving sinner. Verse 5, "*So Jonah went out of the city, and sat on the east side of the city, and there made him a booth...*". When I read this verse, I wondered, who had booths? God directed me back to Leviticus and where He showed me about booths. In Leviticus 23:33-43, and after the children of Israel were delivered out of Egypt and they were in the wilderness, the Lord instituted a feast. He said, *"I want a feast to the booth, and it will last for seven days so that you can celebrate what I've done in your life."* And so here is Jonah in the midst of an angry fit leaving worship going out and building a booth as if he were religious. Even though he didn't have a relationship, he knew how to do church. I know how to say, "Amen." I know how to say, *"Thank you, Jesus."* I know how to serve in a position. That isn't anything but a booth.

He builds his own booth. Let that sink in. Having his own booth trying to create his own space. What is he doing? Processing. I'm going to hold on to religion even though I don't have a relationship. I'm going to be enamored with the name on the church; rather than He, who is the church.

The Lord said, *"That for many, our relationship with God is shaped or misshaped by the experiences of our past."* And so, some of us, instead of continuing in our relationship, we just settle for religion and we build a booth.

Even with his booth building, his booth was not enough to cover him. Psalms 27:5 says, *"For in the time of trouble he shall hide me ..."* You know what he's saying? You can't hide yourself. No matter how hard we try hiding ourselves in a certain church, it will not work. Some of us think if I go to a bigger church, I can hide. You can't hide from God. If I go to a little church, then maybe they won't call on me. He will hide me. Psalm 61:3 says, *"For thou hast been a shelter for me, and a strong tower from the enemy."* Psalm 91:1 says, *"He that dwelleth in the secret place of the most High shall abide under the shadow of the Almighty."* I don't know about you, but every now and again, I need Him to hide me. Hide me, Father. Even if you've got to hide me from myself.

Are You a Self-Serving Sinner

Jonah built a booth trying to practice religion, but he had the wrong attitude. But guess what? Let's read it again, verse 5 says, *"So Jonah went out of the city, and sat on the east side of the city, and there made him a booth, and sat under it in the shadow, till he might see what would become of the city."* Then verse 6, *"And the Lord God prepared a gourd..."* Wait a minute, I've got a bad attitude, God's talking to me, and I am not talking to God. I go on out about my business. I build a booth that can't cover me, and God still covers my disobedient self. God told me to tell you, *"That at your best you are a filthy rag."* So, if God still covered you while you were disobedient, you ought to shout and thank the Lord.

He made a gourd for this boy, and he is in outright, open face, bold face rebellion. God still covered him. You know what He said, *"You don't have enough to cover, so I'm going to cover you anyway."* Then he said, *"You are not enough to save yourself, I'm sending a Savior to cover you when you can't cover yourself. You can't deliver yourself. You can't bring yourself out of this."* What is that? Mercy. We all love grace, but we all ought to celebrate mercy. Why? Because it is new every day. Jeremiah, in Lamentations, tells us that with the rising of the sun, we get brand new mercy. Yesterday's mercy won't do today. God, I messed up again, so I need a new mercy. I've done something I shouldn't have done, so I need a new mercy. I've said something I shouldn't have said, so I'm going to need a new mercy. God, somebody may look at me crazy, and I might get out of sorts with them; so, give me a new mercy because I'm able to mess up.

So, the gourd was given; that's mercy. What has God used to cover you when you couldn't cover yourself? Let's finish verse 6 and see why God gave him the gourd. *"And the Lord God prepared a gourd, and made it to come up over Jonah, that it might be a shadow over his head, to deliver him from his grief..."* Grief? That's a funny word; let's define it. Grief is the pain of mine produced by loss, misfortune, injury, or evils of any kind, sorrow, and regret. We experience grief when we lose a friend or a family member. When we incur loss or when we consider ourselves injured, we grieve. Jonah counted the grace and mercy extended to others as misfortune. Jonah counted God's blessings on others' lives as injury to him. Jonah counted the deliverance of others and sorrow for himself. And this is a servant of God.

Blessings Upon You Indicates His Approval of You

Also, if you believe that God's blessings upon you is an indicator of His approval of you, you might be a self-serving sinner. You think just because you've got the house, God must approve of me. No, you've just got God's grace and His favor and His mercy is on your life. That's not necessarily an indication that God is approving of you. But some of us aren't living two cent worth a nothing, but we are still blessed.

The gourd grew up quick; it didn't take a long time. Some of us know what the law of reciprocity is; you reap as you sow. Through the grace and the mercy of God, we have not reaped what we have sown. We did some dirt and God said, *"I'm not going to let you reap all of it."* He accelerated the covering. Nothing grows that quickly except when God gets in it.

I'm trying to tell somebody who's been looking for some deliverance, looking for a way out, the Lord said, *"It's over; I'm going to make it grow up quick over your life."* Somebody's been waiting and God says, *"Now is the season of acceleration."*

Something can grow up quick. A quick turnaround. A quick covering. A quick deliverance. That's when we say, *"Surely*

Are You a Self-Serving Sinner

the Lord is pleased with me because I got the car." Surely, God is pleased, but then we start riding in pride. I got the car, so surely the Lord is pleased. We got the house, surely the Lord is pleased with us. The house isn't a home, but surely the Lord is pleased. It's the first time I've been to church all year, but surely the Lord is pleased. Throw a rock at a pack of dogs, and the only one that yells is the one that was hit, surely the Lord is pleased.

It says he was exceedingly glad for the gourd. During this whole narrative, we've never heard Jonah mention that he was exceedingly glad in the Lord. Gourd. Lord. Some of us, the gourd is your Lord. You spend more time with your gourd than you do the Lord. He was exceedingly glad. Surely, the Lord is pleased with me. I built my booth. It doesn't matter about my attitude.

Believe God Will Only Comfort You and Not Afflict You

Next, if you believe God will only comfort you and not afflict you, you may be a self-serving sinner. God comforts the afflicted, but He afflicts the comfortable. Look at what verse 7 says, *"But God prepared a worm when the morning rose the next day, and it smote the gourd that it withered."* What came up overnight was gone before the day was done. If you don't give God glory for what God has given you, it can be gone in an instant. If you're giving more glory to the gourd, then you are the Lord, He says, *"You need a worm."* Some of us are dealing with a worm. You know, some of you know about that tequila worm? You don't want that worm.

I want you to understand what is being said here. Jonah did not perceive the worm. It was indiscernible, flying beneath his radar. It was eating away and withering his gourd, and he didn't even know it. I recently taught a lesson about the devil putting his hand in your pocket, robbing you, and you're not

175

aware of what's being taken away from you. I want you to think of that worm. The Lord told me to tell you, "*This worm is time. It's eating away at you, and you don't even know it. I don't care how much you work it out; you think I'm strong, but one day it's coming. Time is eating away at the gourd of your strength.*"

You think you've got a good mind right now? Keep saying good morning. The time is going to come where you get up and go in one room and you can't remember why you went in there. Then you go back to the room where you were so it'll jog your memory. Then you say, "*Oh, I know why I went in there now.*" Keep living because the day is coming when you'll be looking for your glasses and you got them on. Be looking for your phone and you talking on it. "*Lord, where's my phone?*" You pray, "*Father, in the name of Jesus, where is my phone?*" Then the person on the other end says, "*What are you looking for?*" "*I'm looking for my phone.*" "*Well, aren't you on it?*" Lord Jesus, help me!

Withering, all of us. I don't care how well you eat, how much you work out, how much sleep you get when you wake up, you are withering. You might feel wonderful right now, but one day you're going to get up and stuff is going to hurt for no good reason. What is this? Why is my knee hurting? I didn't do anything. I haven't said anything, I was chilling yesterday, and why is my knee hurting? The Lord said, "*If your gourd is withering and your worm is wiggling, and it doesn't work for you, I'll send a wind.*"

The worn Jonah smote the gourd that it withered. Let's continue in verse 8 where it says, "*And it came to pass, when the sun did arise, that God prepared a vehement east wind; and the sun beat upon the head of Jonah, that he fainted…*" There's the law of first mention. I said, "*Lord, where did I hear the east wind first?*" The east wind brought the locusts. But then the east wind also brought the wind that dried up the Red Sea. Some of us think the Red Sea dried up in an instant when Moses stretched out his rod, but it took all night. I'm trying to tell somebody God's sending a wind. Now if it's for you to get right when you know you're wrong, it's not going to be a wind that works for you. It'll be a wind that works against you. You've got to make up your mind. Where is the wind coming from that is blowing in your life in this season? Wind was sent so that he could feel the loss of his gourd. Jonah cares more for gourds than he does for people.

Plants over people. Sound familiar? We love pets more than people. See somebody homeless, and the dog is looking better than the owner is looking. The dog has eaten more than they have. The dogs said, *"Naw, man, you can have that one. I'm full."* We'll stop to pick up a dog out of the gutter, but we better not see somebody sitting in the gutter. We'll drive right past them. I'm talking about us, saints. While you've got that gospel music playing and your air blowing so hard it's disfiguring your face, they're sitting out there in the gutter, and you won't even make eye contact. He just wants something from me. When the Lord had already told you when you were pulling up, give him ten dollars. And you're sitting there thinking, "Nope, I need my ten dollars." That's the devil.

You Allow Passion to Ruin Your Relationship

My last point, if you allow passion to ruin your relationship, you might be a self-serving sinner. Jonah said, *"I'd rather die than to see these people delivered."* You know what that is? Privilege. This privilege is always threatened with equality. I don't mind you moving around me, just don't move next to me, because privilege is always threatened by equality.

Job said, *"The wrath of men kills the foolish man, and envy slays the silly man."* Jonah was asked the question by God. And he never answered it. He just told him I'd rather die. We get to the end of the book of Jonah, and it's open-ended. We don't know what happened. Did Jonah do it, or did he not? Did he finally get it together or did he not? Why did God do that? Because it's left up to us to determine if I am a faithful, full-service servant or if I am a self-serving sinner. What is your gourd? We all got the worm of time. And I promise you since you began reading this chapter, you've lost some time. I know it's hard to hear, but it's the truth.

I'm going to say this; Dr. Benjamin E. Mays said it this way:

> *I've only just a minute. Only sixty seconds in it. Forced upon me, can't refuse it. Didn't seek it, didn't choose it. But it's up to me to use it. Give an account if I abuse it. Just a tiny little minute but eternity is in it.*

He's saying that we are here for a very short amount of time, but what we do in time echoes in eternity. Jesus came, bled, suffered, and died for us so that we will be full-service saints, not self-serving sinners.

Chapter 13
Little Things Make a Big Difference

Ecclesiastes 10:1

Little things make a big difference. There's a concept called the butterfly effect that was derived from the chaos theory that illustrates how small changes in initial conditions can lead to significant and unpredictable results in complex systems. They go on to illustrate it by saying a butterfly can flap its wings in Brazil, and we have a tornado in Oklahoma. It's because everything is connected. Every one of us is connected. So, you must be careful who you connect to.

The term, *the butterfly effect*, was coined by Edward Lorenz who was a meteorologist from the 1960s. He discovered that tiny variations in his weather models brought about incredible differences. In other words, little things make the difference.

It brings us to a place where we look at that in the natural to get a revelation in the spirit. It's a sensitive dependence. This means we are all sensitive to our conditions because none of us likes change, but change is the only constant in life. If you don't believe me, look at your picture ten years ago and look at your picture now. Time has brought about a change. I looked in the mirror this morning and I said, *"Ten years ago, I didn't have gray stuff coming out of my chin."* But time brings about a change. You look at the clothes that you used to be able to wear still hanging in your closet, talking about, *"I'm using that for motivation because time has brought about a change."*

Not only is there sensitive dependence, but there are non-linear impacts. The word *linear* means straight line: but life, is not a straight line. If we're honest, it is filled with crooks and turns, ups and downs, and everything in between. You and I must get adjusted and must come to grips with the fact that life has its own vicissitudes. There are changes and variables, and sometimes we can't keep up with all the changes that are going on. But what do we do? We find the constant in the midst of the inconsistencies and say, *"I'm going to stand right here."* Where is that? You make up in your heart and mind that, *"I'm going to stand on the rock that is my Lord and Savior, Jesus Christ. Even though the winds of change are flowing in around me and sometimes right through me, I'll keep on standing. I'll keep on believing. I'll keep on trusting that my God is able to do exceedingly abundantly above all we can ask or think."*

Not only are their sensitivity dependence and nonlinear impacts, but the Lord says, *"Think about the unpredictability."* This is because we don't know what tomorrow holds, but we do know who holds tomorrow. I was talking to one of the church mothers one time, and she said that she had woken up and her arm was numb. She didn't

Little Things Make a Big Difference

think anything about it and went about thinking that everything was all right, Thank God for daughters because her daughter insisted that she went to the hospital, but because we know how another generation can be a little bit stubborn, she decided she just needed to go lie down. But the daughter insisted, *"No, you're going to the hospital."* So, they took her to the hospital, and they found out that she had had a stroke. What could have happened, thankfully, did not happen. She still has all the faculties of her limbs, she's still here clothed and in her right mind, and glory be to God, she was able to tell me this story. See over the difficulties of our lives and the ways we go through the fire; we need to know that He is the lifter! She was able to come to church and stand to praise God the very next Sunday. The doctor said, *"You had a stroke,"* but then God said, *"No damage, no deficit, and no delineation."* God said, *"I'm raising you up as a testimony. All I'm saying is that small things can make a big difference."*

History is this, Solomon was the wisest man who had ever lived. He wrote the books of Proverbs, Ecclesiastes, and Song of Solomon. When you read those books, you find all kinds of principles and all kinds of precepts for positive living. It's not just a book of quaint sayings and anecdotes, but it is a book of the true and living God. So, if it's a book of God, then we ought to pay attention because then we will live like God wants us to live. I don't want to live with the world on top of me. I want to live on top of the world. I'm able to be in the world, but not of the world. I can overcome it because God is in me. Greater is He that is in me than he that is in the world.

The Pastor's Pen

Small Things that Endanger the Oil, The Opportunist

Let's look at what we can learn about the small things that endanger the oil. First, what we can learn is about the adversary. The adversary goes by many names; he's that old dragon they call him Satan, they call him Lucifer, and they also call him Beelzebub. Do you know what Beelzebub means? It means the lord of the flies.

"Dead flies cause the ointment of the apothecary to send forth a stinking savor..." I want to teach us a little something about, just a few little principles, about flies. First and foremost, flies are opportunists. A fly is waiting to get into your house? They continually fly in this circular motion until they get an opportunity to get into your house. You still think I'm talking about house flies, but I'm talking about temptations and how the enemy keeps flying in a circle. He says, *"I'm flying in a circle because I know Charles is going to open the door in a minute and as soon as Charles opens the door, I'm going to come in his house and I'm going to have my way."* Some of you have a lot of flies that get in your house.

Little things are opportunities to enter your life. He says, *"I'm coming around again."* Do you know what happened with Jesus in the wilderness? The Bible says that the devil left Him for a season. You know what he's saying? *"I'm going to circle around again, and I'll be back. You got rid of me this time. You didn't let me into the house this time, but as soon as I come back, I'm going to get into that house."* He left for a season. So, flies are opportunists.

Do you realize that flies come out of nowhere? I mean, you don't have any flies, and as soon as you put a hamburger on the grill, here they come. Here come the flies getting on your last nerve, looking for an opportunity to get in what you got. You've got to say, *"Lord, I thank you for my blessings but help me kill these flies."*

The lifespan of a fly is about 30 days. Every 30 days, here comes some flies. Have you ever just been in the house and one fly can run you out of your own house? You go after the fly; you are knocking lamps over trying to get the fly. You say, *"I'm sick of you flying past your head."* Buzz, buzz. This fly knows it is messing with you.

Fly Facts

I'm just giving some interesting facts about flies. Flies poop where they land. Somebody said, *"And I ate that sandwich anyway."* You must understand that a fly is on a liquid diet. So, every time they land, they poop. They can't help it; it's just all the liquid. So, they poop a lot. If they landed on it, they probably pooped on it. Let that sink in for a minute.

Flies bringing poop into your life. Walk with me as we take this a little deeper. How many of you had some two-legged flies come into your life and leave nothing but poop? I can deal with some baby poop, but I am not dealing with poop from grown folks. Babies eat strained peas, and you are eating collard greens, and everywhere you go, you leave some poop. If you are not saying "amen," you must be the fly.

Sometimes we think small things don't cause any harm. You see that it just landed on the meatloaf; *"Don't worry I'll just shoo them and just go on and eat."* *"No! No! I don't know where that fly was out there. It's been out in the yard, landing on stuff. Now here it comes flying up in your house."* Buzz, buzz. Leaving trails of poop everywhere it goes. Get them flies out of your house.

Flies multiply quickly. The female can lay 120 eggs at a time, and before you know it, your house is full of flies. Little can become much if unchecked. Jesus said it this way, *"A little bit of leaven will leaven the whole lump."*

Drawing the Flies

Flies live on filth. So, if you got filth in your life, flies are drawn to filth. Pastor, *"I don't know why I keep getting these do-nothing dudes that roll up on me."* Flies are drawn to filth – manure, garbage, animal dung, sewage, and human excrement; that's their jam. So, they only want to hang out where there's some filth. I know what you are saying. I hear you. I'm like my mama, *"I know what you are thinking."* You're saying, *"None of that is in my life."* But if you allow one fly to buzz around, you've got to know that it is bringing something in your life. Because if you didn't have it, where it lands, it leaves traces of it. Where it lands, it leaves traces of it, and there's something you ought to be able to say, *"Wait a minute, I smell something."*

The Apothecary's Oil

From the adversary to the apothecary. Now the apothecary were the ones who prepared the oil. They were the ones that put the scent in the oil. They were the ones who got all the ingredients necessary for the oil, brought it all together, got it all crushed, got it all smelling good, and in the perfect bottle so that it could be used. You and I have a divine apothecary. A divine preparer of the oil. And He must get the container ready to receive it because He doesn't want it leaking out all over the floor because what He wants, He pours in. He wants it to stay in.

Back in the Bible days, I'll just give you a little bit of brief history. They used oil for medicine, burials, lamp fuel, meal

Little Things Make a Big Difference

offerings, and they used it for the anointing and the designating of things holy. So, God says, *"If I've got oil on your life, I have a designation, a distinction, and a difference for your life. Your life ought to be holy."* I know it's not popular teaching, but it's the truth anyway. He said, *"Be ye holy, for I am holy."*

So, those that are single, you have got to take a stance. I know you say, *"It's hard. I don't like to wake up alone."* But you better be careful because that's a fly. Some of you right now have somebody at your house in bed.

He also said, *"The oil represents the Holy Spirit."* So, the apothecary is preparing the oil. And if you and I, declare that we name the name of Christ, we cannot name the name of Christ and be without the oil. I don't want to be naming the name of Christ, and I don't have any oil. I don't want to be in a church where they're naming the name of Christ, and they don't have any oil. You've got to say, *"Lord, I want the oil."* Just know that if He is preparing the oil for our lives, He will provide. Let me show you how the oil was made. Exodus 30:22-25 says, *"There were 500 shekels of pure myrrh."* In order to make oil, the first thing you must have is myrrh, which is bitter. So, I've got 500 shekels of bitterness.

Some of us, we've been through some things. Our generations have been through some things, and we're still trying to wrestle and get therapy concerning some traumas that generations before us had to endure that have been handed down to us, and we don't understand that God says, *"Yes, you have gone through some bitterness. But I'm just making some oil."* Yes, that's why you've been able to overcome it, because God said, *"I've made oil for your life."* Isaiah 10:27 says, *"The burden is lifted; the yoke is destroyed because of the anointing."* The anointing mentioned here is the oil.

So, you have 500 shekels of bitterness, but then the next verse mentions 250 shekels of sweet cinnamon. God won't let everything be bitter without adding some sweet to it. Your life has not been all bitter; you have also experienced the sweetness as well. God says, *"I can't let it all be bitter, because then you would walk away. But I've mixed the bitter and the sweet, so you'll keep on lifting your hands and saying amen and glory be."*

Then the next verse mentions 250 shekels of sweet calamus. So now, the bitter and the sweet, 500 shekels of bitter, right? Then 250 of cinnamon and 250 of calamus, wait a minute, things are balancing out. Where it was once all bitter, He has balanced things out. Now, I've got just as much sweet, as I had bitter. But wait, He's not finished; not only is there myrrh, cinnamon, and calamus, He also included 500 shekels of cassia. What is cassia? Cassia is a spice that is sweet. So, wait a minute. I got 500 shekels of myrrh which is bitter. Then I have 250 shekels of cinnamon, which is sweet. Then 250 shekels of calamus, which is sweet. Then in addition to all that I have another 500 shekels of cassia which is also sweet. So, He said, *"The oil that I produce over your life is two times as sweet as it is bitter."* Hallelujah. I'm just going to talk to myself and say, *"Self, God gave you more sweet than bitter for your life."*

That's 1,500 shekels of oil total. What am I saying? The oil costs. It wasn't cheap. So, if I've got oil, and it costs a lot, guess what? I don't just do anything with that oil. I protect that oil.

The ring your "boo" bought you that costs over $5,000, you don't put that ring anywhere. You have a special place to put that ring. Why? Because it cost. When you had that little two cent worth of car, you were satisfied, but then the Lord blessed you, and now you've got a car that costs $50,000. You don't put that out in the driveway. You put that thing in the garage. Why? Because it cost. So, some of you ladies with all those shoes, you have those things displayed, all of them, especially those red bottoms. They are all on display. Why? Because they cost. You do not have them just thrown in the closet; you know where you have got to find one and then look for the other one. *"Girl, I'm trying to get ready for church, and I can't find my other."* No! You got them right where you can get your hands on them. Why? Because they cost. A man who likes tools do not throw them everywhere. He had spent some money on those tools. Guess what? He got them in a special place, taking good care of them. He has them in one place in the garage. He can open that drawer and immediately know that one is missing. He said, *"Where's my stuff? I put it right here, baby, did you move my stuff?"*

You need to take precautions with stuff that cost, but just know that flies destroy the oil, and what was once sweet, smelling, and wonderful is now stinky.

Do you have a stench in your life? See, oil is not *eau de toilette*; it isn't cheap. Oil costs more. They don't call it perfume; they call it *parfum* because it is not cheap. So, I just wonder, do we have flies? Is there a stench in your life?

Do you need an example? It was a fly of lust that got Samson a haircut. It was the fly of disobedience that lost Saul his position as king. It was that same fly of lust that got David when he looked over there at Bathsheba. It was a fly. The same fly got his son, left his life, landed on his son, and his son had many strange women; 300 wives and 700 girlfriends. All because of a fly.

The Legionary

Flies have been wrecking lives for a long time. So, we have the adversary (opportunist) and the apothecary. Can I call you right now to a new job? The legionary. The legionary is a soldier. A soldier for what? A soldier that comes to guard the oil. God says, *"I make it and prepare it, but you got to guard it. I can't let anybody come and contaminate my oil."*

The scripture said, *"Dead flies cause the ointment of the apothecary to send forth a stinking savour..."* So, the oil was strong enough to kill the fly. The oil is strong on your life. It will kill every fly that comes into your life, but don't let the flies remain. What happens, they died because they messed around and got in the oil. As long as they were around the oil, they could have survived, but they messed around and got in the oil, and the oil killed them. I don't know about you, but that's why I've got to be oily, because some stuff may be landing that I'm not aware of, and it lands on my life, and it cannot stand up against the oil that the Lord has produced over my life. That fly has got to die. He says, *"The oil killed the fly, but they let the flies remain."* Why? Because they think something dead can't cause any more harm. That's why you can't be hanging out with folks whom you once used to hang out with, because you think that relationship is dead, but that thing will rise up and cause you all kinds of trouble. If you don't believe me, just stay in the house with a dead body. I guarantee you; you will move before that body will. The oil killed them, but the flies remained.

I just wonder if there is not a stench in the churches of today. Because there's some oil flowing from the pulpit, there's some oil flowing in the pews, and when flies show up, they die, but we let them remain. We got dead flies sitting in the pews, and sometimes we got dead flies in the pulpits, because the oil of God, you are dead, but you remain and then there's a stench that is coming out of the church. A stench of a bad attitude. You are supposed to be smiling at the door greeting folks. Hey, stench! You are supposed to be standing on the sidewalk, waving and telling people to come on in, but you are standing out there on your phone.

Little Things Make a Big Difference

Who allows dead flies to remain? They are causing a stench, not just at church, but in your life. You know those folks are nothing but dead flies. There are some distinctions when something is contaminated.

I remember a time when we were getting whole milk when the kids were little. Of course, milk wouldn't last long enough to spoil because they drank it, but every now and again, as they begin to get older, we would have to inspect that milk to see if it was good. We couldn't tell until we took the lid off of it and smelled it. What am I saying? We can't tell if some things are contaminated until we get a little bit closer. Anybody can dress it up. Anybody can dance, shout, and say amen but with a closer inspection, when I lift the lid of your life, there's a stench that hits my nose. It has been contaminated. It's corrupted. You've got to get close enough to inspect that thing. You've got to take the lid off. You know what that is? No more cute cliches, *"Oh, I'm blessed by the Lord and highly favored."* I haven't taken the lid off yet. *"I got an increase on my mind, yeah?"* Let me lift that lid. You answer the phone, *"Praise the Lord."* I haven't lifted the lid yet. You are corrupt, chunky milk, and nobody wants their milk in chunks. Preachers got chunky milk. Yes, we know how to give three points and a poem and close with an ah, ah, ah, ah, ah, ah, ah, ah. But let me lift that lid. Let me see if there's some real oil there. Is there a stench? The stench of pride. The stench of arrogance. The stench of self-righteousness. What's going on under your lid? Because it's easy to say it about the preacher, but what about the pew? You are prideful. You are self-righteous. You are arrogant. Got malice and strife and envy all in your heart. I'm lifting your lid! There's a stench in the body of Christ. Hatred dressed up in patriotism. As if God is dressed up in red, white, and blue. God isn't American.

The church is guilty of this, too. We have a bad taste in our mouths; we desire bigger buildings, but not better believers.

The Pastor's Pen

We've got a bad taste for increasing our numbers on social media. We've got a bad taste for followers. We don't develop disciples just as long as they tune in and I can say, "*I got 3,000 watching online.*" Why? I wear a $1,000 suit, a man bag and gators for the haters. We want to perfect the website. We want better musicians, so we pay them more. We'd rather be an influencer than a God-called preacher. A bad taste because if you're God-called, you don't care what anybody says. I don't care how you roll your eyes; I'm going to tell you the truth anyway. We have so many preachers who are now trying to build a brand and promoting self instead of promoting Christ. It's all about their brand, but where is Christ?

I remember when I was starting out in ministry, they used to ask me, "*Is it going to be Larry Charles Ministries?*" I quickly said, "*No! Because I knew if it was Larry Charles Ministries, then I'm depending on Larry Charles who is insufficient to try to do that which only the All-Sufficient One can do. It isn't my ministry; it's the Lord's ministry.*"

So, when it isn't cars and cash and clothes, where is your ministry? I'm talking to you too, saint. It's not just going to church and sitting in the pew and going home and don't give a dime. Sitting, looking, soaking up all the air and you don't do anything; yet, trying to judge everybody around you. Get off of your do nothing. I'm lifting your lid, and it stinks.

There are many that desire to become a millionaire, but you don't give a dime in church. God says, "*If you're not faithful over a few, how can I make you ruler over much? You are a thief.*" You get $10,000 at once and give the church $100. What! And still think God going to bless you? I'm trying to see if I can really trust you. You don't know what God is doing in your life. He's trying to see if He can trust you with a dollar. Give me a dime out of that, and you have refused. So, He says, "*Okay, you going to be in want because if you don't work on the principle, you are going to need a miracle."* Because we don't have a thirst for truth anymore, we've got a thirst for things.

The Ostiary

We have the adversary, the apothecary, and the legionary; let's talk about the ostiary. Now the ostiary is a word that was used originally for an enslaved person. Let that sit in for a little while. It was originally used for an enslaved person or a guard posted at an entrance of a building. They were the ones with responsibility and the authority of keeping the door. God is calling you into duty today. He's calling you to be an ostiary, to stand at the door as a guard for your oil, protecting it from the flies coming in and contaminating it. There will not be a stench in my oil. My oil shall flow and flow freely down the corridors of the time that I am walking in. When I walk, I leave oily footprints. When I lay hands, I leave an oily handprint. Because the Lord has called me for such a time as this. So, if I'm a doorkeeper, the door is a place of transition. It's a place of discomfort. Because when we're in transition from one place to another, there is nothing to support my flesh. I'm wondering, where is my next foot going to fall? And I'm talking to somebody in this room who is wondering just that, *"Lord, what's next?"* But the Lord told me to tell you, *"I create doors and I will create a way where there was once no way, and it won't take me six months, nine months, or a year to make a door appear. I can make a door appear in the moment, right now."* Somebody, a door can change. You can lift your hands right now, and a door can open for you. You can open your mouth and begin to magnify the Lord, and a door will open for you. You've got to be able to say, *"Lord, yes, it's me, Oh Lord, I magnify Your name. I glorify Your name. I say hallelujah to Your name,"* and as you are in the act of worshipping Him, God can open a door.

The Pastor's Pen

You don't get from where you are to where you want to be without going through a door. So, God says, *"I'm making you the ostiary. I'm making you the doorkeeper."* You've got to find the door then, brother. You've got to find the door then, sister, and declare nothing that God doesn't want to be in my life can come in my life.

When you go to Walmart, they've got a set of doors that you walk up to, and they open for you. I'm trying to paint the picture because the Lord says, *"When you pulled into the parking lot, that door was opening for others because they were in the right place."* When you get to the right place at the right time, the Kairos (the appointed time), not the Kronos (quantitative time); the God-appointed place in your life, you won't have to force the door open. He said, *"Just keep on walking and the door will open."* Somebody ought to declare, *"The door is opening today."* This is the day my door opens because I feel like something in the spirit is leading me to that place to be able to declare that the door is opening for me.

Let me talk to the real believers because the Bible says, *"If you've got Jesus, Jesus is the anointed one."* So, if I've got Him in my life, I don't have to worry. I've got enough oil for the situation I'm in and the flies can't stand up to that oil. Beelzebub can't stand up to that oil. The lord of the flies has got to bow to that oil. Why? Because that oil, according to Isaiah 10:27, *"…and the yoke shall be destroyed because of the anointing."* The anointing in this verse is the oil. Every yoke shall be destroyed because of the oil.

According to Isaiah 61:1, *"The Spirit of the Lord God is upon me; because the Lord hath anointed me to preach good tidings unto the meek; he hath sent me to bind up the brokenhearted, to proclaim liberty to the captives, and the opening of the prison to them that are bound; To proclaim the acceptable year of the Lord…"*

Little Things Make a Big Difference

Psalms 45:7 says, *"Thou lovest righteousness, and hatest wickedness: therefore God, thy God, hath anointed thee with the oil of gladness above thy fellows."* Who am I talking about? I'm talking about Jesus. My rock in a weary land, Jesus. My shelter in a time of storm, Jesus. My bread in a starving land, Jesus. My water in dry places, Jesus. He is the way, the truth, and the life. His name is Jesus. He's Wonderful. He's a Counselor. He's the Mighty God. He's the Everlasting Father. He's the Prince of Peace. He's the Great I Am.

A fly is a little thing, but Samson used a little thing like a jawbone, and he slayed a thousand. So, flies can be used for the bad, because it's a small thing. But the Lord said *"You can use something small for something good."* He said, *"If Samson could use a jawbone, then David can take a smooth stone, one smooth stone, and slay a giant that others couldn't stand up against."* Jesus took two fish and five loaves of bread. A small thing, but He was able to do something great with it and then there were three nails. One in the right hand, one in the left, and one through His feet. Only three small nails, but glory be to God. It brought salvation. It brought religion. It brought redemption. It brought sanctification. It lifted up the bowed down head. All because of three small things. Give God praise; small things can make a big difference.

Chapter 14
The Truth About Trouble

2 Corinthians 1:8-11

"*For we would not, brethren, have you ignorant of our trouble.*" I pray that as I share this, you will be blessed. I'm uncomfortable giving this confession, but I've been instructed by God that I must confess. I am in an entanglement. It is a relationship that I don't even want, but it is yet and still a relationship. She came into my life a long time ago, and she comes and goes from time to time. Sometimes she shows up for half a day. Sometimes she shows up for an extended stay trying to rekindle the same feelings of insecurity and fear. She likes multiple partners; black, white, Jew, Gentile, Protestant, Catholic, male, female, and others. She's no respecter of persons. She even visits me and my wife from time to time looking to create a soul tie and trap us both in her web of misery and pain. She is a merciless pursuer and even Jesus warned us of her in John 16:33. Her name is Trouble.

The Truth About Trouble

While you sit reserved reading this right now, I know she has visited and is visiting some of you right now. Whispering in your ear, telling you about what you can do, what you can't do, and what God won't do or what He will not ever do in your life. But you've got to look at Trouble and say, *"Get thee behind me, Satan; the Lord rebukes thee."*

Join me as I take you on a journey. Get in the car of your choice: Mercedes, Volkswagen, Hyundai, Honda, Cadillac, Porsche, or Bentley. Whatever it is, truck, car, bicycle, come on and ride with me. If you have a window, I want you to roll it down so that you can hear the sounds and see the sights. As we go down this dusty and winding road to the place called Asia, her town is like any other. This town Trouble lives in has its own post office where people write about her. It has its own church where preachers preach about her. It has its own center and a school where teachers teach about Miss Trouble.

They tell them that sooner or later in your young life, there's going to be some trouble. And I don't care how good you are, I don't care how big your Bible is, I don't care how many scriptures you can quote or how much oil you got in your purse, every one of us is going to have to deal with some trouble. We join Paul in 2 Corinthians as he's writing to the church of Corinth, telling them about his missionary journey. While he is talking about his missionary journey, he tells them that God is the Father of mercies and the God of all comfort; that's in 2 Corinthians 1:1-3. By the time you get to verses 8 through 11, he begins to unfurl that he has had some trouble. Even the great apostle had some trouble. So, if somebody who wrote the Bible had trouble, I think those of us that read the Bible just might have a little bit of trouble. God shared with us how to deal with troublesome times. We should not get discouraged, but we need to hold on to what He is doing in the midst of our troubles. No matter the situation, we've got to hold on. Politics often make people uneasy, but God said, "*I don't care who's in the White House. You better recognize who's on the throne.*" There is something happening across this country and if you are not careful, you will be asleep at the wheel while all of this stuff is going on around us. You've got to say, "*Lord, help me to keep my eyes open. Let me be vigilant. Let me be sober. Don't let me be duped by the things that people tell me. But Father, I want to know as Pilate, what is the truth concerning the things that are going on in this world today?*"

Facades Disappear and Faith is Developed

So, what happens to us, as we go through trouble? Let me just give you a couple of things. Number one, when you're in trouble, facades disappear, and faith is developed. No cute cliches when you're in trouble long enough. No more, I'm blessed and highly favored. No more, I'm too blessed to be stressed. No more, I'm the head and not the tail. Now, your wig is twisted, and you don't know where your phone is because you are in trouble. You don't want to hear nobody with a '*hey diddle diddle, the cat and the fiddle.*' I don't need a poem, but I need a word from the Lord to encourage my heart and lift my spirit. I'm about to lose my mind and you're talking about '*the cow jumped over the moon.*" I need a word from God.

The facades disappear and faith is developed. What happens? My confession is my honest feelings. I'm going through, but I know the Lord will make a way somehow. But right now, if I'm honest, "*I'm going through a little something.*"

Sometimes when people are going through, they don't have to tell anyone because it can be seen on their brow. Those with the spirit of discernment can see that the enemy has had

The Truth About Trouble

you on the run, and that trouble has now shown up and she's got her bags with her. She's got Louie with her. She's got all of her bags and they've been pushed up to your door and is expecting you to take them in because she plans to be there for a while. You heard what the doctor said, Trouble has moved in. You heard what they said on your job, Trouble has moved in. You feel how you feel in your body; Trouble has moved in and is refusing to leave. You look at your children and you see, Trouble has moved in. You look at your grandchildren and you say, "*Oh, God, here comes Trouble.*" You look at your great grandchildren and you say, "*Lord, I know Trouble is coming their way.*"

As I encourage you, I want you to know that the Lord told me to tell you, "*Yeah, you're going to have tribulation in this world but be of good cheer because I have overcome the world.*" Just know you can trust Jesus. Anything written in red, I'd put my foot on it. It's a firm foundation. You've got to say all other ground is sinking sand, but there's no other name. Paul said, "*I wouldn't have you ignorant.*" Why would he say that? Because many folks look at the glory, but they don't know the story. They see the car you drive now, but you don't see the car you had before. They see the house we live in now, but you didn't see where we lived before. You don't know what we had to endure to get to where we are. Blessed be the name of our God that He made a way when there was no way, that He opened the door when there was no door, that He brought light into the midst of darkness, and He gave me strength in the midst of my weakness. If it had not been for the Lord.

Despite all that God had done, many still come with a facade because they are not in a personal relationship with the Lord our God. How dare you come with your cute cliches without saying, "*Lord, You've been good to me.*" We need to have a heart of gratitude and adoration and praise. We need to come before the Lord and say, "*Lord, I thank you for Your kindness."* Paul said, *"I've got to confess because you see glory. But you don't know the story."* We don't know the fullness of what one another had to go through to get to where they are now. So, he said, *"I don't want you to be ignorant, just without knowledge."*

He didn't say *"ignant"* because that can't be fixed; however, ignorance can only be fixed with proper information. But if you're *ignant*, you're just *ignant*. I'm sorry, but I know some *ignant* folks. Paul said, *"I wouldn't have you ignorant about the trouble which came to us in Asia."* What's in Asia? Verse 8 continues by saying, *"...that we were pressed out of measure..."* That word *pressed* is *'bereo,'* which means to carry a heavy, heavy load. Have you ever tried to pick up something that you know you can't pick up? You struggled with it and then you might have taken one step and dropped it and couldn't pick it up again. That's the kind of burden Paul is telling us that he was under.

Some of you are under a lot of pressure right now. That word *pressed* means to be under pressure, under the weight. It pictures a beast of burden who collapses under the weight of its circumstances. Now, we know a beast is supposed to be able to carry the weight. A beast is supposed to be able to endure the weight. But the beast stumbled and crumbled under the weight. There are some of us today that are stumbling and crumbling under the weight of what it is that has been put upon you. The trouble is so excessive that you say, *"Lord, I don't know how much more of this I can bear."* But the Lord said, *"Just take another step, daughter. Just take another step, son. Yes, I'm going to bring you out when others said you'd never come out. I'm going to bring you through when others said you were through."* Hold fast to your faith and say, *"If it had not been for the Lord on my side,"* as Paul said. He said, *"I was pressed beyond measure. I was pressed, and under a heavy, heavy load."* Being felt as

The Truth About Trouble

though he was being pressed and crushed; he says, *"It was pressed out of measure."* Measure comes from the word that means thrown beyond expected boundaries. It's thrown out of bounds; even though it's out of bounds, it still means that you're in the game. We think out of bounds means the play is over. But no, God said *"When there's trouble, you can be out of bounds and still be in the game."* Yes, I've been pressed, I'm out of bounds, but I'm still in the game.

Paul said, *"...pressed out of measure..."* You know, when it's out of bounds, it's out of sight, and you feel it shouldn't be happening to you. You know, I go to church every Sunday. Some of us have to press our way to get to church some Sundays. In the rain, glory be to God. The scariest time for a preacher when he hears thunder on Sunday morning because he said, *"Lord, they aren't coming."* But I the preacher am glad to see the saints that press their way to the sanctuary on a rainy Sunday morning. Why? Because you said, *"No matter what, I'm going to press my way because I believe there's something for me in the sanctuary."* David said, *"I was moved by the foolish, but until I got to the sanctuary."* He said, *"When I got in the sanctuary, then I understood."* He said, *"I was wondering why people who were evil, prospered; while those who were righteous, seemed to be going down."* In other words, he had put his eyes in the wrong place. You have got to keep your eyes on the Lord in this world we live in because the enemy would love you to lose your focus so you could possibly lose your life by thinking about the wrong things. By comparing ourselves with others and thinking, this shouldn't be happening to me. But the Lord said, *"Why not you?"* Because we think it ought to be happening to somebody else. Or we think it could never happen to us. But the Lord said, *"Why not you?"* I know it's a turbulent time right now, but the Lord said, *"Don't worry. The facade is disappearing, but the faith is being developed."*

The Pastor's Pen

Verse 8 says, "*...that we were pressed out of measure, above strength...*" You are being pressed out of measure, beyond your strength but your faith is being developed. The strength that is being developed is an amazing strength that is above and beyond any other strength known.

I thought just being pressed was enough to describe that I couldn't handle what was going on. But he said, "*No.*" There's another degree because even though we may grab a hold of something that's heavier than we can handle, we still think we're smart enough. You say, *"I'm smart enough to deal with this because I matriculated at the university, and I've got a degree on my wall. I drive a nice car. I've got some nice shoes. I live in a nice neighborhood."* But guess what? Trouble still knows your address.

Above strength is beyond the human ability or power to cope. So, my education won't get it. My intellect won't get it. Paul, knowing multiple languages won't help because I can't talk my way out of this. My connections. My companions. None of that works in this situation. It doesn't matter about your homeboy. It doesn't matter about your homegirl. They can't fix this. You're going to have to get it straight in your mind that you need Jesus.

Pressed out of measure, beyond our strength and he said in the final part of 2 Corinthians 1:8, "*...we were pressed out of measure, above strength, insomuch that we despaired even of life.*" Despaired of life. A loss of will to live. Things can get so heavy, and things have not been going your way for so long, we know them, and we see them but do not know how to cope. We see examples of this in the world we live in, and many have come to a point where they lose the will to live. Robin Williams made us all laugh but, on the inside, something was not right. He may have felt hopeless. Smokey Robinson said it best, "*The tears of a clown when no one's around.*" How many of us go to church, shout "*Hallelujah*," and go home and cry yourself to sleep? Because your joy is based on where you are, not whose you are.

He said, *"We are despaired of life."* Paul was saying, *"I gave up."* What? Not the Apostle. Not the one who saw Jesus on the Damascus Road, not the one whose tongue talking, not the one whose scales fell from his eyes, and not the one who hears God speak to him directly. He said, *"I despaired of life,"* because depression was real. I'm despaired of it, and I didn't want to be here anymore. And yet and still we're just having in church while somebody next to you is in a place of despairing life.

You have the nerve to sit down and not speak to the person sitting next to you. Your smile may be the only thing that will help them make it another day. How many times have we heard a wife say about her husband who took his own life, *"I never even saw it coming. He seemed like he was okay; we were just celebrating our anniversary."* Or she says, *"I just left and took the kids to drop them off at the movies and I come back, and this is what I find."* Could it be that we are not tapped in like we ought to be? We don't even ask one another if we are okay. We're sleeping with him, and we don't even know him.

When you are able to confess your inability, that's when God shows up with His all-sufficient ability. Paul's confessing was him saying, *"I am despaired of life."* You know what he was saying? He was saying, *"I'm so weak that I can't do it, but God can."* He was giving God glory by telling his real story. No facades, just genuinely crying out to the Lord sharing his internal feelings.

Confess Rather Than Complain

The second point I'd like to share is that we ought to confess rather than complain. I walk through the halls at work every day and see people weak. I see people being emaciated by the disease, I see them losing their faculties and, in some instances, their dignity, and we have the nerve to complain. God told me to tell you, *"If you grumble about your situation, you have lost your focus."* If you have the nerve to complain, he says, *"You have lost your trust because you are saying I don't even believe God can deliver me from what it is I'm going through."* Complaining means you want to be glorified, but confessing means I want God to be glorified.

We hear Paul say a lot, but we never hear him complain. Have you ever found yourself singing that old time song that says, *"I've had some good days, I've had some hills to climb, I've had some weary days and some sleepless nights but when I look around and I think things over all of my good days outweigh my bad days, and I won't complain."* Hallelujah. I won't complain because I want Him to be glorified in my life.

Are you a complainer? Or are you a confessor? Where do you stand in your walk with God?

Self-Revelation Over Self-Preservation

The third point I'd like to share is self-revelation over self-preservation. At the end of 2 Corinthians 8, it says, *"...insomuch that we despaired even of life:"* Verse 9 continues by saying, *"But we had the sentence of death in ourselves, that we should not trust in ourselves, but in God which raiseth the dead:"* In other words, our backs were so firmly pressed against the wall that we thought, this is it. We had the sentence of death in ourselves.

Have you ever thought? I don't know how this is going to work out. I guess we're just going to lose everything. Then in the midst of your situation and your back against the wall,

The Truth About Trouble

God found the space between you and the wall and intervened. Listen, Paul says, *"We had the sentence of death in ourselves and that we should not trust in ourselves."*

Wait a minute, let's take a closer look at what is being said. When he says, "We should not trust," you mean to tell me; I'm going through so that I can learn who I need to turn my trust to. Isaiah 26:3 says, *"Thou wilt keep him in perfect peace, whose mind is stayed on thee: because he trusteth in thee."* So, does this mean that I'm not getting perfect peace if my trust is not intact? So many place their trust in the wrong places such as their job or their bank account. This is why some fail to give. Others trust in their spouse. We should not trust in ourselves. That means he was trusting in himself. Like us. Leaning on the gift rather than the giver. I have to be careful that I don't begin to think that I'm all of that and a bag of chips and forget to say, *"Lord, have mercy on me."*

We live our lives in drive but matters of faith, they're realized in reverse. You can't see the hand of God until you look back. Once God has brought you out, then you look back and you reflect retrospectively and you say, *"I see God's hand right there. I saw it in who He sent to me. I saw it in what was said to me. I saw it in what they did to me. If it had not been for you Lord."* But you didn't see it until you looked back.

Paul looks back, let's look at what he says in verse 9, *"But we had the sentence of death in ourselves, that we should not trust in ourselves, but in God which raiseth the dead:"* That's gangster talk. That's when you say, *"I may die, but He is going to raise me up again."* That's Daniel and the Hebrew boys. They said, *"O King, we're not careful to answer you concerning this. But guess what? You can play all the music you want to play, but we are not going to bow. And the God we serve is able to deliver us. But if he doesn't, we still are not going to bow."* That's gangster. I don't care what anybody says; that's real gangster right there.

In Genesis 8:2, Noah built an altar and sacrificed and worshipped God after finding dry ground. What was that? That's a retrospective kind of offering. God, I'm blessing You because You blessed me. You brought me and my family through the storm and the rain and the heartache and the pain. I heard others drown to death, but God just saved me and my family.

In Genesis 28:16, while Jacob was on the run from Esau, he laid down in a field and used stones as his pillow. And while he was sleeping, the Bible says that there was a dream that was given unto him. In that dream, there was a ladder that reached from the earth into the heavens, and there were angels ascending and descending and above that ladder stood God Almighty declaring, *"I will bless you."* But when he woke up, he said, *"This is the house of God, and I knew it not. I didn't know it until I looked back retrospectively. I couldn't see the revelation until I looked back. I couldn't feel the power until I looked back. I couldn't understand the anointing until I looked back."* But there was something that God brought him through that made him realize, *"I now know that this is the house of God."*

He didn't say it was a building. It was a place, and some of us can mark a place in our life that we say that was God's resting place. That was God's dwelling place. That was the place that God opened the door. I'm a witness; to declare, it was the place. You can't see it until you look back.

In Judges 16:28, Samson's eyes have been gouged out. He was bound and grinding in the meal like an animal and the Philistines say, *"Bring Samson out because we want to make sport of make fun of him. Where's your great strength now, Samson? Where's your God now, Samson?"* But Samson has been contemplating some things. Because remember when he had Delilah, she says, *"Where does your great strength lie?"* He told her a bunch of mess before she got on his nerves so much and revealed to him that his hair had never been cut.

They bring Samson and he said, *"Show me where the pillars are."* The little man leads him and shows him where the pillars were, and Samson prayed. Samson said, *"God, give me strength."* Wait a minute, you said your strength was in your hair, so why are you praying to God for strength? Why? Because he didn't have a chance without eyes to see what he couldn't see when he had eyes. Sometimes it takes the loss of something in order for you to see. Keep on acting foolish. Keep on doing what you're doing. Keep disrespecting your mama and your daddy. I guarantee you; you're going to lose something, and then you're going to be able to see what it is you have lost. You have got to look back so you can see.

He said in verse 2 Corinthians 1:10, *"Who delivered us from so great a death, and doth deliver: in whom we trust that he will yet deliver us;"* Who delivered us, that's past. Then he says and, which is a conjunction that means there's something else coming. Doth deliver, that's present tense. So, he has delivered. He is delivering. Then he says in whom we trust that He will yet deliver. My God has delivered, is delivering, and He will deliver. I don't care what you're going through. If He's done it before, He'll do it again. Same God way back then, same God right now. Hebrews 13:8 says it this way, *"Jesus Christ the same yesterday, and today, and forever."* There are levels to this.

God Is Still Doing Something

My next point is even when it seems that God is doing nothing, God is still doing something. I know you need Bible because you are all Bible scholars. Think about the life of

The Pastor's Pen

Joseph, from a pit to a prison. Scholars say he spent 10 to 12 years in prison for something he did not do, and it didn't seem right when he thought he was going to get out when he helped the cup bearer and the baker. Joseph prayed, *"Lord, give me a revelation about the prophecy, regarding the dreams of these individuals."* He received the revelation and shared it with them with only one request, *"Don't forget about me when you get back up and get your position. Don't forget about it. Come back down here and holler at your boy."* But this didn't happen until two years later, and Pharaoh needed one of his dreams interpreted, and then they remembered Joseph. The Bible said two years went by. Why didn't God give the king a dream before the two years? Because when it seemed like God was doing nothing, God was still doing something. What was He doing? He was working on Joseph's heart. He said, *"Joseph, I can't let you hold the grudge."* Because some of us, when he showed up in prison, would not have nice things to say. They would probably say something to upset Joseph, such as, *"I know it's been two years since I saw you, but I'm trying to get in good with the king. Can you just come on and tell him some stuff that you told me?"* Some of us would have said, "Boy, if you get closer to these bars, I'm going to choke you." He said, Joseph, *"I've got to deal with your heart."*

How about the children of Israel in slavery? The Bible shares that they cried out because of their taskmasters. Still got the whip on their backs. Still having to be in the brickyards. Still got mud between their toes. But when they cried out, God didn't seem like He was doing anything to help them. It didn't seem like He was doing anything, because He was over in Midian talking to the answer. He had to go to Midian and talk to Moses and say, *"Moses, take your shoes off for the ground on which you stand."* They had prayed in the brickyards. But God was moving in Midian to get the answer to come to them. And somebody reading this right now, the

The Truth About Trouble

Lord told me to tell you, *"Even though it seems like God is doing nothing; don't worry, there's a Midian."* God is speaking to the answer and if that isn't enough, while we were yet sinners, Christ died.

Intercession and Thanksgiving

So, the last point, there has to be some intercession and some thanksgiving. Because so many of us are so ungrateful. Just a bunch of ingrates. Just entitled and spoiled and we fall out on the floor and kick and holler when things don't go our way. You know what that used to get me? My mama used to tell me, *"The place you show out is the place I'm going to show up."* I'm upsetting your sensibilities. Parents today say, *"That's so barbaric. We don't do that anymore to our children. We send them to time out."* But my mama said, *"I will knock you out."* She didn't have to do it; the threat was enough. You know what? I trusted in Mama because I knew she would do what she said.

Paul says, in verse 11, *"Ye also helping together by prayer for us, that for the gift bestowed upon us by the means of many persons thanks may be given by many on our behalf."* So many of us, only pray for me, my four, and no more. Me, my five, and we are trying to stay alive. Me, my six, and we watch the devil and his tricks. Me, and my seven, and we on our way to heaven. But we don't intercede for the church service. Intercede for your pastor. Intercede for the first lady. Intercede for anyone by ourselves. Saints, it's time to pray for the body of Christ, for our country, for the world, not just those in your immediate circle. Saints, today I admonish you to activate an active prayer life, giving God thanks. When you intercede, Thanksgiving is the result. Thank you, Lord, for the doors you've opened. Thank you, Lord, for the ways you've made. See, somebody prayed for me; they had me in mind. Somebody is praying for you. I thank God for the saints that have gone on to glory that had taken the time to pray for me.

We see in Genesis 18:16-33 that Abraham intercedes for Sodom. Exodus 32:11-14, Moses intercedes for Israel. In 1 Samuel 7:5-9, Samuel intercedes as the prophet for the nation and for Israel. John 17, Jesus intercedes for His disciples and the coming believers. That's you and me. *"Lord, I pray that You'll send Your glory. The same glory that You shared with Me before I came into this earth. Share Your glory with them. Lord, I thank you that I can leave My peace with them."*

Many of us never pray for anybody because intercession is a behind-the-scenes kind of thing and we want to be recognized. You don't attend intercession prayer meetings, you don't get on the Wednesday night prayer calls, but now, Pastor wants you to pray in service and here you come with your Pharisee prayer, trying to impress somebody with your words.

So, Paul says, *"that for the gift bestowed upon us by the means of many persons thanks may be given by many on our behalf."* Because when you pray for somebody and then they come back and tell you the Lord has made a way, they give thanks unto God for the intercession.

You and I ought to be thankful unto God for our Savior and for the Spirit of the Living God. For when we don't know what to pray, the Spirit intercedes on our behalf with groanings and mutterings that cannot be uttered. He makes a way out of no way for us. And we know that way is a bloody way because Jesus bled, suffered, and died. But thanks be to God, He rose on the third day with all power in His hand. And now you and I have a right to the tree of life.

The Truth About Trouble

This is the truth about trouble. Where are you today? If you're in the midst of trouble, He says, *"I'm the burden bearer. I'm the heavy load sharer. I'm the midnight rider."* Somebody's caught in darkness, and they can't feel their way out. You can make it, my brother. You can make it, my sister. All of us have made some mistakes, but I'm so glad we serve a God who says, *"I cast your sins into the sea of forgetfulness, and I remember them no more."*

Chapter 15
Don't Reject the Invitation

Matthew 22:1-14

Don't reject the invitation; rejected invitations can be costly. The year was 2008, and Google offered a company by the name of Digg two hundred million dollars for their news platform. Digg rejected the invitation. This digital news platform could have been sold at that moment if they had just accepted the invitation for two hundred million dollars. But they rejected the invitation. Later on, they were able to sell it but only sold it for five hundred thousand dollars. Any mathematician can determine that there was a hundred and ninety-nine million five hundred thousand dollars left on the table.

Brothers and sisters, in my opinion, Digg stands for "*Dumb, Ignorant, Goofy, and Gonna be kicking yourself.*" I have missed out on a hundred and ninety-nine million dollars if only I had just accepted the invitation. I'm not just talking about consequences in time that can be costly, but I'm talking about eternal consequences. Every time we reject an invitation from our God and our Savior, we are putting ourselves in position to suffer eternal consequences. Time is marching right along, and we are going along. Many times, we are going along to get along, but what we have to realize is I don't have time to reject any invitation sent by God. Rejecting an invitation from God is one thing that would cause us to miss eternity.

Neglect

The first point I'd like to make is it is not materialism or our love for things. It is not heathenism or love or pleasure and self-indulgence. Brothers and sisters, it is not even atheism that you believe that there is no God. The thing that is detrimental to each and every one of us when we're talking about the invitation of God is simply neglect.

Lady and I often get gift cards to restaurants from our friends and loved ones. When we get these little gift cards, we put them away and say one day we're going to go and we're going to enjoy that, but right now we don't have time. We'll just pick it up at another time. There have been times we've left money on the table because we have simply neglected to receive the invitation. We laid it aside and we looked at it every now and again and said, "Yes, one day we're going to do that, but we can't do it this weekend." Then we realize oh the next doesn't work either. Before we knew it, one weekend turned into two and two turned into ten and now it's a year later and we decided to use it, but now it's expired. We missed the opportunity because of neglect. Not because somebody shunned us, we knew it was there, but we just disregarded it.

Such is us in the House of God, many times we miss what God has for us because we neglect it. We neglect the calling and the assurances that God has provided for us because we are negligent in seeking out the face of God. We have got to say, *"Lord, am I negligent in the things of You? Have I missed You because I'm hardheaded? Have I missed You because I've been indulged in other things? God, am I a negligent believer?"*

Jesus tells the parable, of an invitation given, but also an invitation rejected. He tells us of the preparations that have been made. He tells us that there was no expense spared in the preparations. He tells us that when all things are prepared, He sends forth His willing servants to call those that have been extended the invitation to come. For all things are now ready. Our God has gone away to prepare some things for us. And He said, *"If I go away, I will come again unto you."* He says, *"I'm already extending the invitation."* Every invitation that we receive is an invitation that has been given in the past for a future event. We're all invited to a future event. God's getting us ready for that great day. We don't have time to play, and this is not a time to reject the invitation of our God, but to prepare us for the future event.

Let me talk about this invitation. It arrives in the mail, and it's on linen paper with gold embossed imprinting upon it. It has calligraphy letters; it is a fancy invitation. It's like you get an invitation from the White House, and it is in all kinds of lettering, and it has the presidential seal on it. But brothers and sisters, the invitation we've been given came in an embossed envelope with gold lettering and the signet ring seal of the royalty upon it. We have an invitation from the king, Hallelujah!

At Harry and Megan's wedding, I guarantee you those that got the invitation still have the invitation because it showed up and it was fancy. That was not an event that they were going to miss. Those invited gladly accepted the invitation because this is a once in a lifetime opportunity, and I just want to let somebody who has not made Jesus their Lord this

Don't Reject the Invitation

that is a once in a lifetime opportunity. It won't come after this. You've got to make up in your mind and say, *"For God, I live and for God I'll die. I'm going to humble myself to seek the face of God, for without Him, I can do nothing but through Him all things are possible."*

During those times, when an invitation to a wedding was given, they would send two invitations. They would send the first one to let you know, "Save the date." It would be all fanfare and all of this, and then they would send the second invitation when all things were ready. Not only would they send two invitations, but with that invitation would come a wedding garment. The wedding garment would come because there would be people from different social and economic stages, and so they wanted everybody to feel like they were a part of the wedding party, so they wouldn't have anyone looking down on one and looking up on another so everybody would be dressed the same. When we come to Jesus, there aren't big '*I's*' and little '*you's.*' It's not going to be pastors over here and bishops over there. No, all He says is servant. As He looks around the room, He is looking for the servants that can say, *"I've got my wedding garment on. When I come before God, I'm not coming like I got all the pomp and the circumstances, but I'm humble and meek as a lamb. For without Him, I don't have a garment at all."*

There's a language of the invitation that says, "*Your presence is requested.*" The company of your presence is requested at the event. Brothers and sisters, every time you go to the house of the Lord, your presence is requested. He says, *"I didn't come here for you to see what I'm wearing. I came because I serve a risen Savior. I came because of the Holy Ghost. I came because He raised me because He turned me around. He placed my feet on the solid ground. I came not because of my own strength. I come today because if it had not been for the Lord on my side, I never would have made it."*

The Pastor's Pen

Formal invitations show the guest what they can expect at the event. They show how you should be dressed – it's formal, semi-formal, or business casual. They give you information on the invitation. The Bible says, *"Let whosoever will, let him come."* That's an invitation right there. Whosoever I just know, I'm in the whosoever. The attendees, the attire, and the food; there's some information. He said, *"I've prepared a supper."*

When I was coming up, my mother taught me it was breakfast, lunch, and dinner. But then I went to the country. And they used to say, *"Yes, this is breakfast."* And then when we get to lunch, they say, *"This is dinner."* I was like, *"No, this isn't dinner; this is lunch."* They would correct me and say, *"No, this is dinner."* I said, *"What's this evening?"* They said, *"That's supper."* I said, *"Supper?"*

So, when we're talking about the marriage lamb. He said, *"This will be the last meal."* See you think you've been eating on this side; it's been good on this side, but the Lord said, "You have not seen anything." Greater. I can't wait to get there because I believe we're going to be able to eat and not gain a pound. Give me some more greens and cornbread. Give me some more of them candy yams. Come on baby, give me some more peace cobbler with some of that Blue Bell ice cream on it. We'll be able to eat and not gain a pound.

In 1 Peter 2:9, it says it this way, *"But ye are a chosen generation, a royal priesthood, an holy nation, a peculiar people; that ye should shew forth the praises of him who hath called you..."* That's an invitation. He had called you; that's in the past. He said, *"I have already called you."* Have you rejected the invitation? He already told you who you were. Now He's calling you to a new place in Him. He says, *"Why have you rejected My invitation?"*

Don't Reject the Invitation

Zephaniah 1:7 says, *"Hold thy peace at the presence of the Lord God: for the day of the Lord is at hand: for the Lord hath prepared a sacrifice, he hath bid his guests."* He says, *"I sent you an invitation."* He's wondering who is going to respond. Have you RSVP'd yet? Some of us don't even know what RSVP is. It means there is a response requested and expected from you because of the elaborate happenings and the event that are being prepared, we need to know if you will be in attendance. Most invitations request your response on your meal choice. Do you want chicken, fish, or beef? Someone just shows up based on what they say they're serving. I'm not going to see so and so, but I'm going to get some meat.

Revelations 19:9 says it this way, *"And he saith unto me, Write, Blessed are they which are called unto the marriage supper of the Lamb...."* Blessed are they who have been invited. You and I, we've been invited. What I'm saying is, every time we come here there's an invitation. Every time you sense the conviction of the Holy Spirit, it's an invitation. Every time the Word leaps off the page and slaps us upside the head, it's an invitation. He's trying to get you to turn yourself around.

Refusing the Invitation

He sent the invitation and when it was time to call them to come, they refused. They refused, and so do we. We go to church week after week, month after month, year after year. We hear the word, then we get up, go about our lives, and never do it. It does no good to hear it and never be a doer. We are instructed to hear and obey.

Preparation

Now let's look at the preparations. While making the preparations, He said all things are ready. Not some things, but all things. I remember one time we went to a birthday party that was supposed to start at four. We get there at six and they were still cooking. When I left home at four, which was a two-hour drive, I said, *"I want to get there and be going through the line with my plate."* When I arrived, I was smelling smoke. I thought, *"Why am I smelling smoke? It should have been done."* But that's us, all things are not ready. We still hopping around the store and trying to wrap up things, yet we are not ready. Do you know what time it is? It's getting late in the evening and the sun is going down. You supposed to be prepared by now. Y'all still think I'm talking about that birthday party, but now I'm talking about us, we should be ready by now. In Jeremiah 8:20 it says, it this way, *"The harvest is past, the summer is ended, and we are not saved."* See, you should have been ready; you should have had your business fixed. An old songwriter used to sing a song *'It's Nobody's Fault but Mine.'*

All things are ready. In other words, you didn't have a hand in this. He says, *"This is not something that you will be able to help me do for you."* Like some of us think. We think we're all that and a bag of chips. Some of us showed up, and we are going to be able to check a box, "I went to church and Jesus ought to just be happy that I went to church."

All things are now ready. Notice the first time, He said, *"Compel them to come that I invited."* They rejected it. This next time, He says, *"Tell them what I got ready."* He was thinking this would make them want to come. We see it in verse 4, *"Again, he sent forth other servants, saying, Tell them which are bidden, Behold, I have prepared my dinner: my oxen and my fatlings are killed, and all things are ready: come unto the marriage."* They didn't eat a lot of meat back then, so they would jump at an opportunity to have meat. Oh, they got meat over there. That's how they doing it; we are going.

Don't Reject the Invitation

The Bible says in verse 5, "*But they made light of it, and went their ways...*" You know what was keeping them? It wasn't that they didn't have the proper garments; it wasn't that they didn't have their hair done nor their nails done or their wig tight. What kept them from coming? They were not hungry. So many of us, we fill up on so many other things. My mother used to tell me, when she was cooking and I said, "Mom, I'm hungry," and she said, "*I'm not going to let you get anything right now because it'll spoil your appetite.*" Somebody knows what I'm talking about they have a mama like mine. No, I can't let you eat that, because if I give you that, you're not going to want this. Some of us got too much of that and we don't want this. He says, "*They were not hungry so they would not come. Too busy filling up on Real Housewives of Atlanta and other distractions that keep us from accepting the invitation and acting accordingly.*"

We get full of the world, and we don't have room for God. So, it didn't matter that it was a sumptuous presentation or the greatest chef. It didn't matter that everything was in line and perfect for them because they were not hungry. Jesus said, "*They that hunger and thirst after righteousness shall be filled.*" Where are the hungry ones? Where are those that say, "*I have got to get more Jesus. I'm hungry for Him. I want a greater revelation, I want deeper insight, and I want filling of the Holy Ghost because I know I can't live without it. I don't need cotton candy. I need Jesus.*"

Where is the meat of this situation? He said, "*Prepared the meat for you.*" Some of us were too immature. He said, "*I want to give you meat, but you aren't ready for it. So, I'm going have to give you milk.*" But the king said, "*Come, I've got milk and meat for you. I got what you need, just come.*"

The fatting calf, the oxen, the best of the best, have been prepared. You do know God is not taking any shortcuts? He's an extravagant kind of God. He gave us a sign of it when they had two fish and five loaves of bread, but after everybody was fed, they left with twelve baskets. That's an extravagant God. He gives us more than enough. In Ephesians 3:20, it says, *"Now unto him that is able to do exceeding abundantly above all that we ask or think..."* He says, *"I'm an extravagant kind of God, and I'm always doing more than you can ask for."*

Don't settle for less than the best. These things are meticulously prepared. In 1 Samuel 16:1, the Lord is speaking to Samuel and asking him, *"How long wilt thou mourn for Saul, seeing I have rejected him from reigning over Israel? fill thine horn with oil, and go..."* If the Lord was saying to fill my horn, that means I have emptied my horn. That means I have poured oil in places trying to get somebody else to do what is right. Samuel had exhausted all of his oil dealing with Saul. There are many that have exhausted all of their oil dealing with some frivolous relationship and some foolish person. He commanded Samuel to prepare because a new thing is coming. He said, *"Don't get stuck on what was, but walk with Me now."* Just know that the more I walk with God, the more oil He gives me. It's time for you to confess to the Lord, *"I'll walk with You because I want to leave some oily footprints. I want some oil, God, for lifting the burdens. I want some oil, so we can destroy a yoke. I want some oil because without the oil, I won't be able to do what You called me to do. Without the oil, God, no burdens will be lifted, and no yoke will ever be destroyed. God, I need Your oil."*

Proverbs 22:3 says, *"A prudent man foreseeth the evil, and hideth himself* (he prepares): *but the simple* (fools) *pass on, and are punished."* If you fail to prepare, you prepare to fail. If I didn't study, if I didn't fast, and if I didn't pray, I failed to prepare. Guess what? Sunday morning, I'm preparing to fail.

Don't Reject the Invitation

I will never be what God wants me to be, except that I seek His face. If you're going to sing, you need to prepare. If you going to read a scripture, you need to prepare; at least read the scripture silently before you get up before everybody. It will keep you from stumbling all over the words and if you don't know a word, pick another scripture.

Confrontation

OK, there's invitation. There's preparation. Now, I want to get to this part that the Lord blessed me with, He said look at the confrontation. In Matthew 22:5, *"But they made light of it, and went their ways, one to his farm, another to his merchandise:"* We see that life is filled with the confrontational priorities. There's always something vying for our attention, pulling us to the left and pulling us to the right. Where we think we've got to make more money, or we've got to get this money. We can't go to work or go to church on Sunday or Tuesday night. We are trying to get this bag, but we have misaligned priorities. But we are instructed in Matthew 6:33, *"But seek ye first the kingdom of God, and his righteousness; and all these things shall be added unto you."* He says, *"If you keep Me first, I'll make sure everything else works out."*

The Lord told me to tell you, *"You've been rejecting His invitation, but you need to make Him first."* You've been seeking everything else, but God said, *"If you ever put Me first, I'm going to make everything line up. If you put Me before your family, if you put Me before you, I will work it all out. If you can do these things, I'm going to make everything line up in your finances and your romances. I'll make it all line up because I am the Lord. I am the Lord thy God."*

I'm struggling because I got misaligned priorities. What's your farm? What's your merchandise? Priorities. I'm still in

The Pastor's Pen

Matthew 22:5, but let's look at the parallel account of this is in Luke 14. There are three individuals. One of them is what I call indifferent, he outright says, *"I'm not coming. I don't care what you say, Jesus. That's fine, but I'm still not coming. But praise the Lord for You."* We've got indifferent folks all around. Man, you ought to come on and go to church. Come on and see what the Lord is doing. Then they respond by saying, *"Well, preacher, I am not coming, but I'll get your church a donation."* In other words, *"I'll pay you to get outta my face."* Indifferent, no particular interest, no sympathy, unconcerned because they don't realize that the invitation that is being extended is not from me but from God.

The second type of individual is the indisposed. Not only did they refuse to come, but they were also unwilling to come. They had other things to do. Now this is where we are at in Luke 14, because there are three people there. One said, *"I just bought some property, and I need to go and look at it."* Does that sound strange? Do you buy something before you look at it? He said, *"I bought it, now I've got to go look at it."* Oh, you're a fool anyway. You need Jesus now.

Not only that the second one said, *"I just bought some oxen, and I got to go try them out."* You know how you get a new car? You don't come to church on Sunday? You've got to go and ride. My mother used to say, *"You've got some gas on your chest, don't you, son?"* What she meant was, you want to ride, don't you? Then she'll follow up with, *"You got some money, 'cause I ain't gonna buy you gas."* I would respond, *"Yeah, Mama, I got some gas money."* I had five dollars, but a dollar went a lot further back then. I could ride all week on five dollars. Try that now, and you'll be on the side of the road calling your mama and saying, *"I ran out of gas."* He said, *"I've got some oxen, and I have to go try them out."*

Then the third one responded saying, *"I got a wife, and we just got married. I can't come."* You know what he's doing?

Don't Reject the Invitation

He is using the Word to justify his reason for not accepting the invitation. Since you're religious, you understand religious talk, so I'm going to share with you the law in Deuteronomy 24:5 where it says, *"When a man hath taken a new wife, he shall not go out to war, neither shall he be charged with any business: but he shall be free at home one year and shall cheer up his wife which he hath taken."*

I tell married couples the Bible says that you are to stay with her for a year, no separation. Some of our marriages are in trouble because we never spend any time together. Here you are saying you're a Christian, but you got married and immediately got on the road. If you don't spend some time with your wife, there's going to be some distance between the two of you. You'll be wondering, why does she not respond to me in the way she used to? Because she doesn't know you like that anymore. You've got to stay close to your wife.

The third type of individual is the indicted. Let's look at Matthew 22:6, *"And the remnant took his servants, and entreated them spitefully, and slew them."* I'm talking about an invitation rejected. They attacked the servants of the king. I just wonder how many you know are blaming the servants of the king. It's that preacher; he's the reason I rejected the invitation. They have a mindset that *'ain't nobody no good anyway.'* They lump all preachers into one category thinking all they want is their money or all they want is to sleep with all the women in the church. They point the finger and blame others, those in service to the King for their shortcomings, all while being unwilling to surrender.

Church should be a place where we come together corporately to learn about the great mysteries in the Bible and draw closer to the Lord. We don't come for it to be like an auction. God does not bless based on who gives the most, especially if the giving is only to be seen by others. Remember, He sees your heart while you are giving.

Manipulation, don't fall for it. I want you to be free. Just know that John 8:36 says, *"If the Son therefore shall make you free, ye shall be free indeed."* Know that without God, there is no freedom, no liberty. It gets on my nerves when people try to blame some servant whom they encountered and this servant did wrong, and then they paint with the broad brush thinking that every other servant is the same way. Everybody is not a Jim Baker. Everybody is not Jimmy Swaggart. Even when they went through, the Lord is still using them. They are people who make mistakes, but we shouldn't say everybody is like that.

Devastation

There's the invitation, the preparation, the confrontation, and for my last point, there is the devastation. What happens when we reject the invitation given to us by God? Devastation. Matthew 22:7, *"But when the king heard thereof, he was wroth: and he sent forth his armies, and destroyed those murderers, and burned up their city."* The Lord told me, *"Some of you are suffering right now in your place because of how you rejected the invitation of God."* And even his servants listened because you don't have to pull out a gun and shoot a sermon, you can kill him with your mouth.

You kill the pastor with your mouth at Sunday dinner. Did you hear what Pastor said? Pass the pot roast. "What scriptures was he reading?" Rejecting the invitation and it says, *"...he burned down their city."* Some of you smell smoke. Your place is on fire. What was their place? All the things that kept their attention and focus were all gone. They thought it would never pass away; yet, it was gone in a day.

Don't Reject the Invitation

We have to realign our priorities to make the Lord the center of our lives.

How many people have put all their money in stocks and bonds, and the stock market crashed, and everything that they had built up was gone? In a day. A reputation can take years to build, but it can be ruined in a moment. One moment and nobody will ever forget; we have to know that people are not forgiving. In the church even. We shoot our wounded; we kill them dead. *"Oh, you got wounded out there, pastor." "Well, I'm sorry,"* pow.

Their place was burnt down all because you rejected the invitation. Everything they thought would last forever was gone. I was working with a lady, and they fired her. She'd been there since the beginning, which was over twenty-two years. When they took her job from her, everything she had depended on was gone and she lost it. She literally lost it because she was not rooted and grounded in Christ. She had a confession, *"I love the Lord. The Lord is good, and His mercy is everlasting. His truth prevails."* These were her faith confessions as long as things were the way she wanted them to be. But when things shifted, it revealed that she was not as rooted as she claimed to be.

It's the same way for all of us. We can confess when we got enough in the refrigerator and when we got money in the bank. When we've got some stocks and some bonds and we got something to lean on. When your 401K is in good shape or when you matriculated at the right school and everything is the way it ought to be. Your baby is a well. What about when the doctor says that your baby has a sickness that they have no cure for? What about when you have a special needs child and your husband decides this is not what I signed up for and walks away? You're going to find what foundation you're really standing on. See if you're standing on the rock.

You'll be able to stand when the rains are coming, and the winds are blowing.

It says in Matthew 22:7-9, *"But when the king heard thereof, he was wroth: and he sent forth his armies, and destroyed those murderers, and burned up their city. Then saith he to his servants, the wedding is ready, but they which were bidden were not worthy. Go ye therefore into the highways..."* This is the third invitation. God is constantly pursuing us. He is constantly watching out for us. You may be at home upset and mad about something that didn't go your way. He didn't answer my prayer. And then you are flipping through the television and the preacher says, *"The Lord said..."*, and you say, *"Oh, turn that off."* What is going on? He's pursuing you. You lay down and take a nap and have a dream and you say, *"Woah, what was that?"* He's pursuing you. If He can't reach you through the medium of television, through the medium of the Internet, or the medium of your phone, He said, "I'll meet you in your dreams." Why? Because He says, *"I'm pursuing you. You are mine, and I love you with an everlasting love."* We have to determine if it is the Lord, are we responding to or rejecting the invitation?

Now he extends another one to those that were in the highways. This is a representation of the Jewish people who rejected God. He says, *"I'm going to the Gentiles."* And if for any of you reading this now trying to determine if you are a Jew or a Gentile, let me tell you, you are a Gentile. You ought to thank the Lord that He came to your highway. I'm on the outskirts, but He still came and found me. I wasn't just in the highway, but I was in the alley. Some became weakened right there because they didn't want to admit they were in the alley, too. See, you were in the alley. Some of you may say, *"Well, I had a nice upbringing. I had my mother and my father, and we had everything."* This is all great, but what is

Don't Reject the Invitation

your relationship with God like? Yes, you may have had everything, but you were in the alley with God. Hard-headed alley. Disgruntled alley. He goes out and pursues them until He finds them. He said to go get them. Why? Because time is winding up, and one day the door of grace that is on God's Banquet Hall will be closed.

Remember the five foolish virgins in Matthew 25? They came and the door had already been shut. And they said, "Open the door," and Jesus didn't open the door. He didn't look out or open the peephole, He said, *"Depart. I don't know you."* Every time I read it, I shudder because I don't want to be in a place where I'm standing before the door and grace has closed on me. In other words, there'll be a time where you will pray, and it won't do any good. He's closing the door from the day that you and I came forth screaming from the womb. The door of grace began to close just a little bit.

They have the atomic clock; now it's at a minute to midnight which means that we are closer than we ever been to Armageddon. Some folks are like well, it's been a thousand years, but a thousand years is as a day with God. And a day is a thousand years, so He's not concerned about time. He's concerned about His purpose.

Well, it was the place, it was the people, and it was personal. He says in Matthew 22:12-14, *"And he saith unto him, Friend, how camest thou in hither not having a wedding garment? And he was speechless. Then said the king to the servants, Bind him hand and foot, and take him away, and cast him into outer darkness, there shall be weeping and gnashing of teeth. For many are called, but few are chosen."* He comes in to look at the servants. The wedding was furnished with guests, and when the king came to see, not if, but when the king came to see, he came to see the guests. As he looked and there was a man at the table who didn't have a wedding garment on. And the king looked right at him, and said unto him, *"Friend, how comest thou in hither not having a wedding garment?"* And he was speechless. Why do we always try to show up as if we're going to outdress somebody else? All of them wearing them robes, but I'm going come in my Brioni. I'm going to wear Prada tonight. I'm wearing Donna Karen. I'm going to show up with my red bottoms on. So, we think we are better dressed than what the host has provided. So, what he shows up in is self-righteousness. He thinks when he shows up, he's going to kill them because he's got the "baddest" rags on. That's us. We're thinking that we're better than everybody and we're more righteous than others, when the truth is we need to pray more, read our Bibles more, and get to really know the Lord. Thinking we are better than others is self-righteous and prideful; a Pharisee. Just because you've got a few passages highlighted in your Bible, you're so busy looking at the next person who can barely find Genesis in their Bible, and you think you're better than them. You better be careful who you're dealing with these babies you don't know who God has His hands on.

He just decided, *"I'm going to show up; bump the garment you provided. I don't want to wear that. What I'm wearing is better. Your garment is cheap. Look at the lining on that; mine has paisley in the lining and goose feathers. I'm all that and a bag of chips."* Preachers can be self-righteous. That spirit can attach to anyone. Self-righteous preachers may think nobody can preach it like they can preach it. We want to holler and 'ain't' said nothing. He said, *"I'm coming to the feast, but I'm coming in my own righteousness."* We come to church in our own righteousness. We mount the pulpit in our own righteousness. We sing the songs in our own righteousness. We pray the prayer in our own righteousness. You sit and look at the preacher with a blank stare in your own righteousness. And God says, *"You're rejecting the invitation."*

Don't Reject the Invitation

The host said, *"How did you come up in here not having a wedding garment?"* And there was nothing he could say. Why is he speechless?

First, he's speechless because he couldn't say, *"Well, I couldn't afford it,"* because it was provided. Salvation is free. It's already provided.

Secondly, he could not say he didn't need it because he definitely needed it; something was missing in his life. How many of us have ever felt that something is missing, because we have not been draped in the robe that God has provided for us? We want to come to the supper, but we can't come in our own strength. We've got to come saying, *"Lord, it's to You and You alone I cling. I cling to thee because anything else is sinking sand. On Christ, the solid rock I stand. All other ground is sinking sand."*

Thirdly, he could not say that he did not know about it, because when he came in everybody else in the room was wearing it. Like some of us. All the people in your family who know the Lord are telling you, *"You need to get right with Jesus."* Instead of you embracing it, you reject it; be careful. You may not get another opportunity.

Finally, he could not say that it was too hard for him because Jesus made it really easy when He said, *"Come onto me, all ye that labor and are heavy laden and I will give you rest."* It's an invitation.

I'll end with this story. There was an elderly woman on her sick bed. She was in hospice. She had been a faithful believer her whole life. One of her great grandchildren was sitting there with them and he looked at her and said, *"Grandma, are you afraid to meet death?"* She looked at him and with her weak voice and a smile on her face, she said, *"I'm too well dressed to miss that."* She wasn't talking about her bedclothes; she was talking about the robe that the King had provided. Barring Jesus is coming back. I'm going to give you a stark reality. Barring the coming back of Jesus, one out of every one of us is going to die. You just better make sure you got the right robe on.

www.ingramcontent.com/pod-product-compliance
Lightning Source LLC
Chambersburg PA
CBHW070643160426
43194CB00009B/1560